classic jazz

Arranged by Brent Edstrom

Cherry Lane Music Company
Director of Publications: Mark Phillips

ISBN 978-1-4584-0533-3

Visit our website at www.cherrylaneprint.com

BAG'S NEW GROOVE

By MILT JACKSON

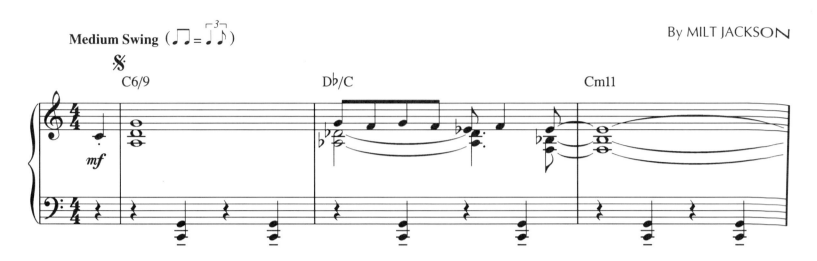

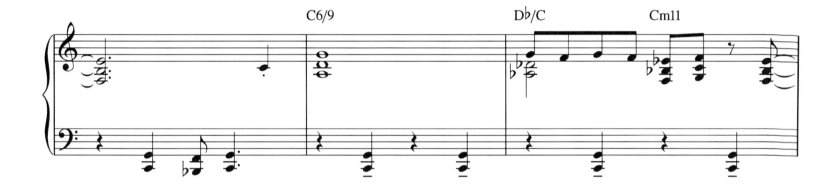

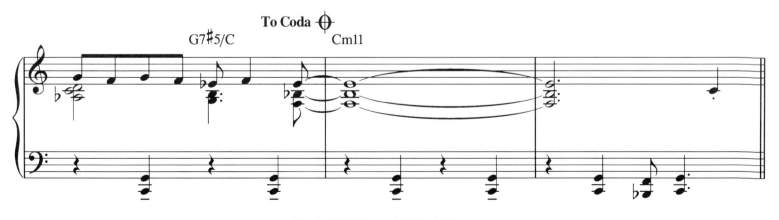

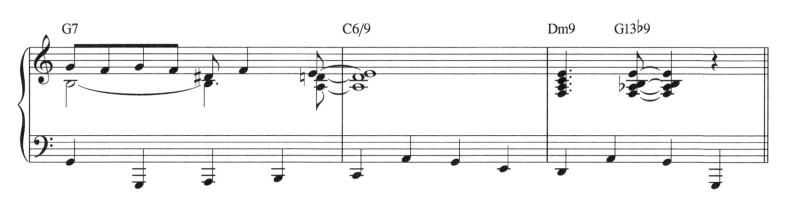

4

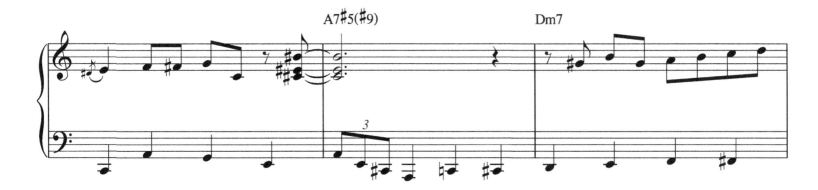

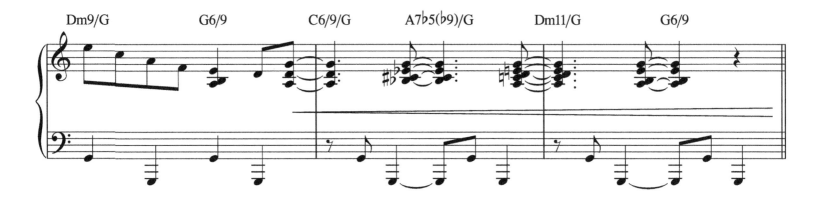

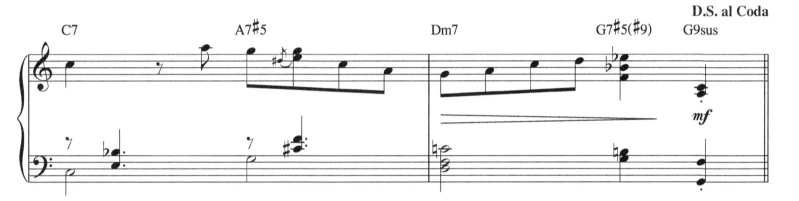

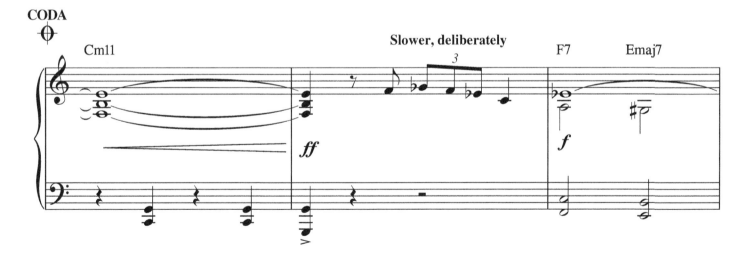

BLACKBERRY WINTER

Words and Music by ALEC WILDER
and LOONIS McGLOHON

Ballad

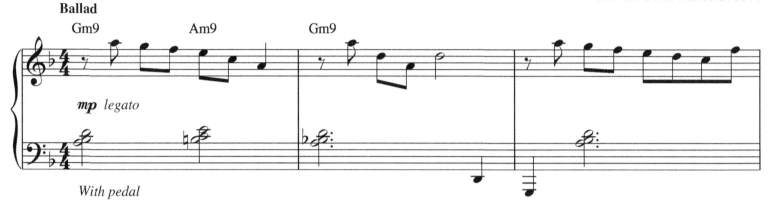

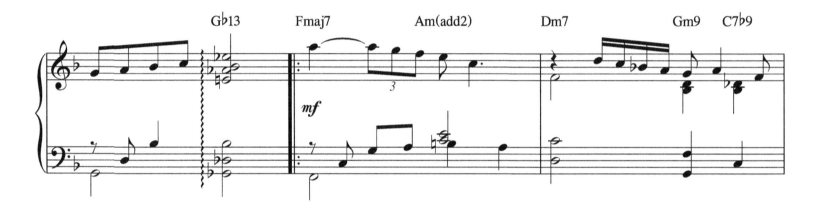

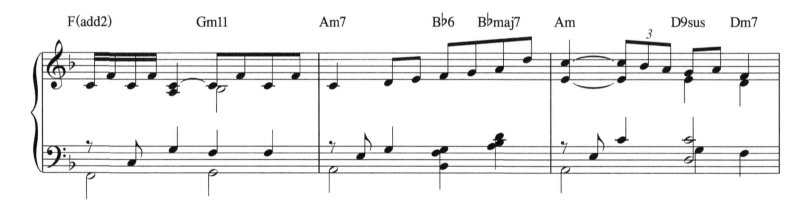

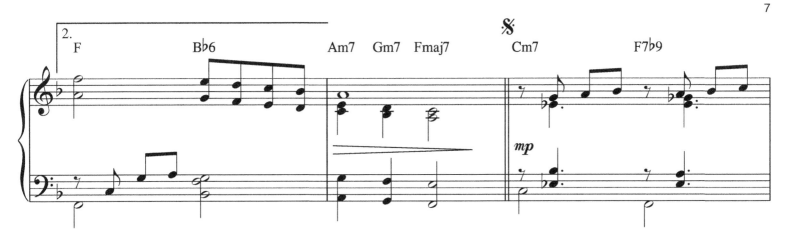

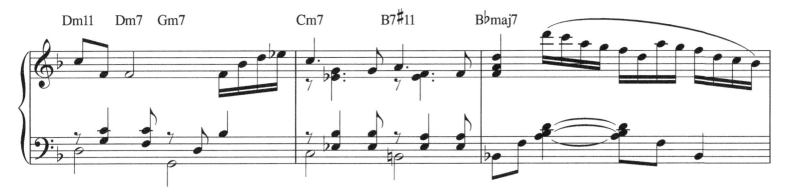

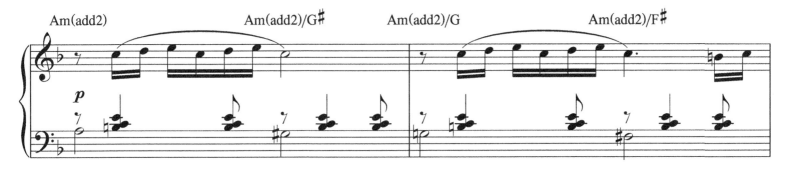

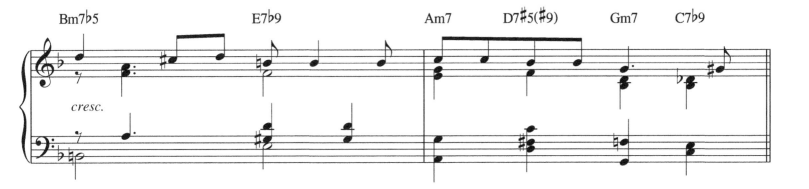

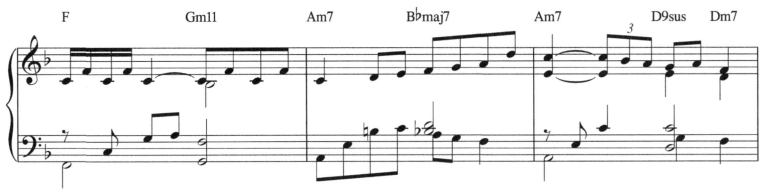

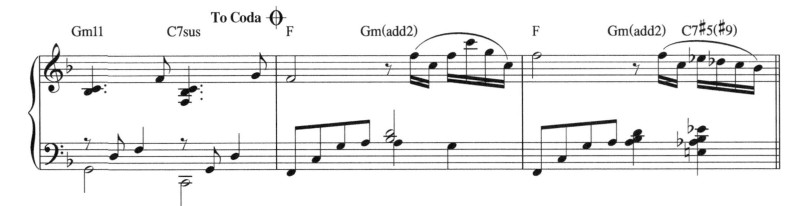

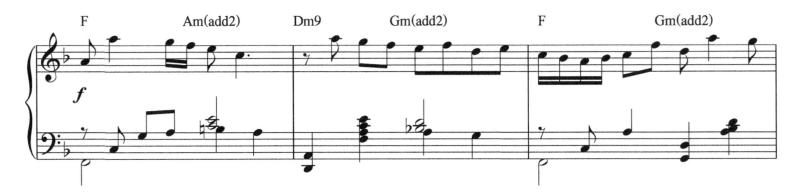

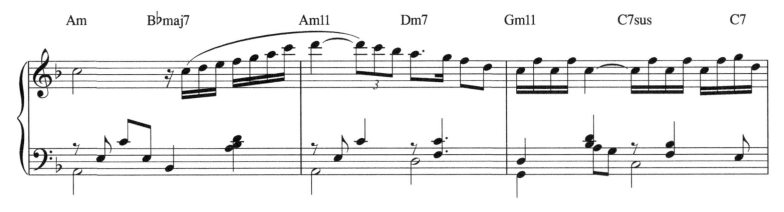

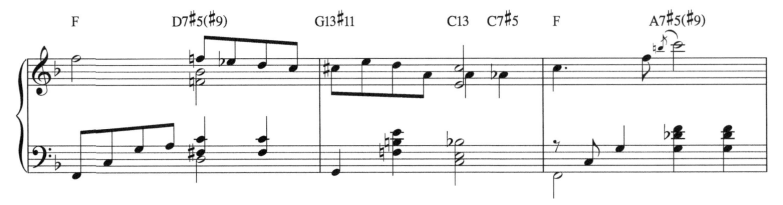

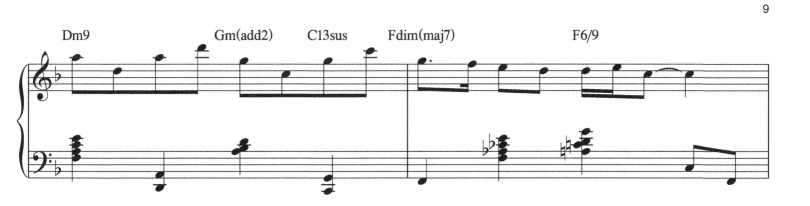

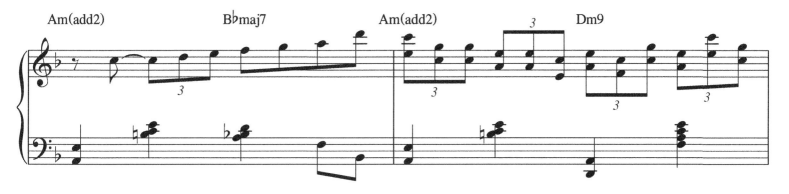

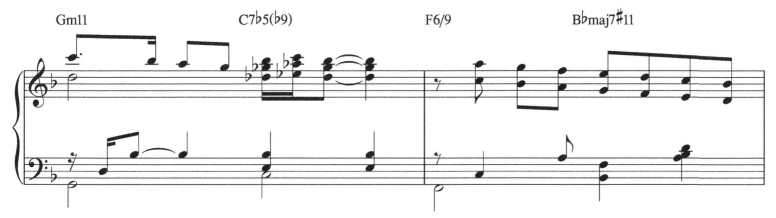

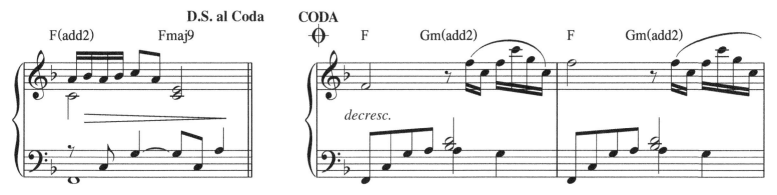

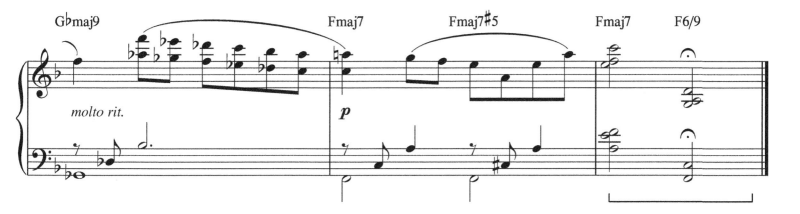

BOUNCING WITH BUD

Words and Music by EARL "BUD" POWELL
and WALTER GIL FULLER

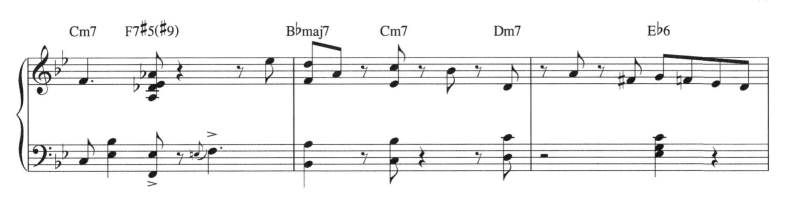

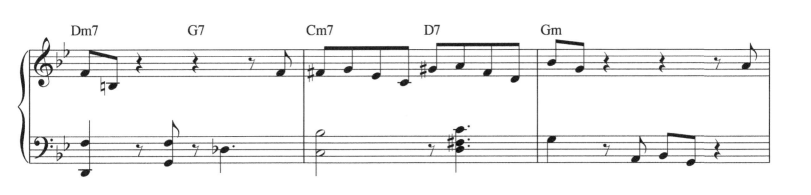

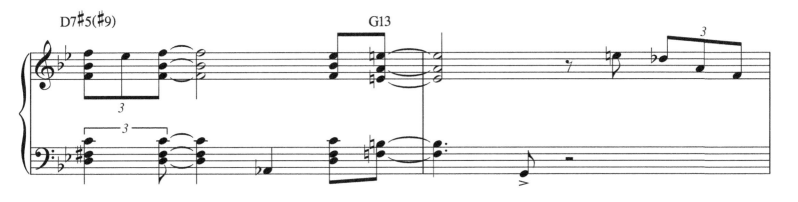

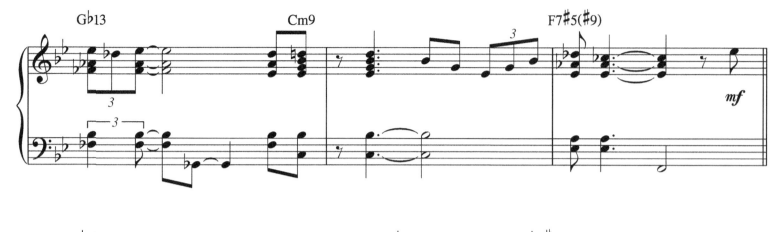

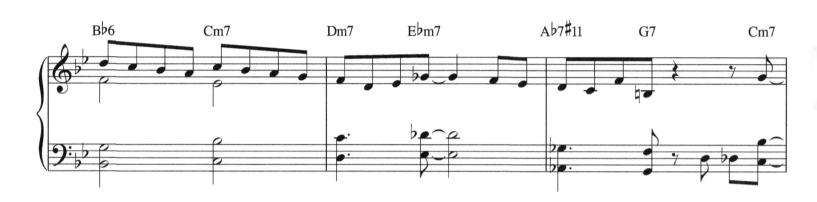

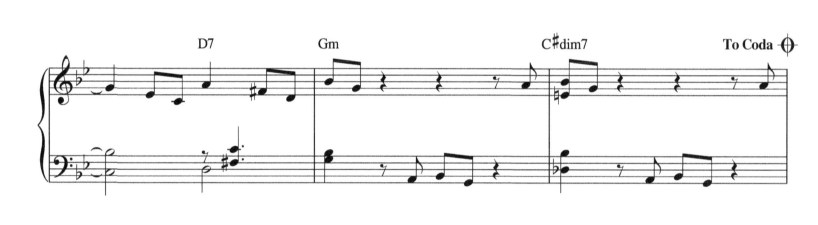

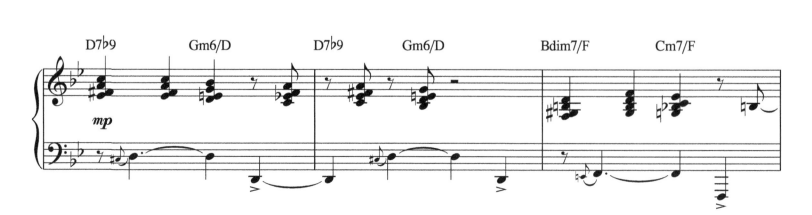

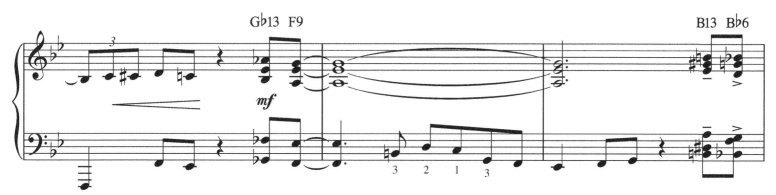

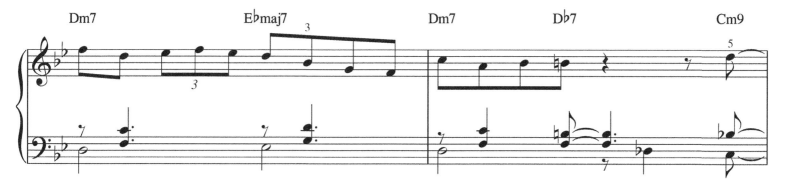

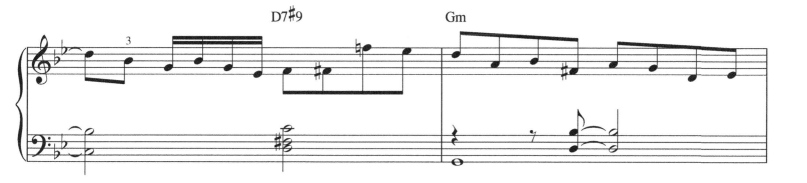

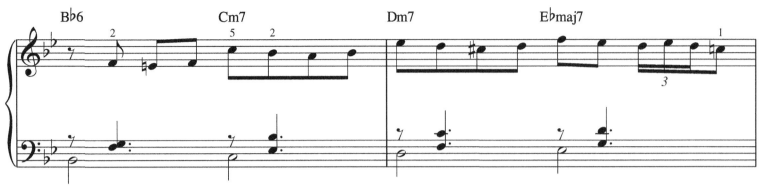

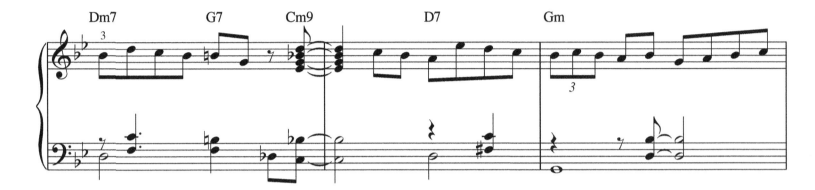

DOLPHIN DANCE

By HERBIE HANCOCK

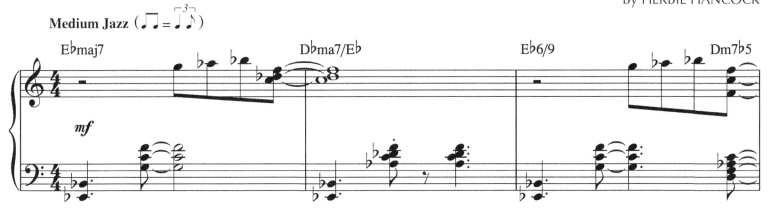

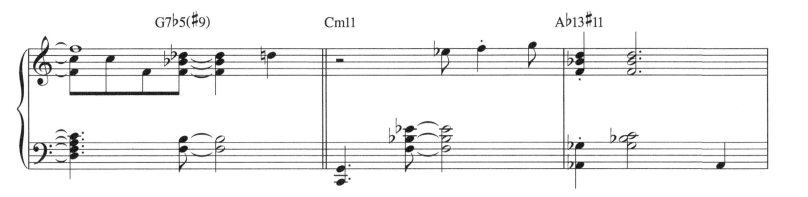

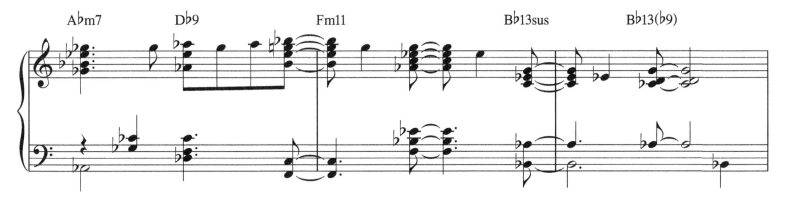

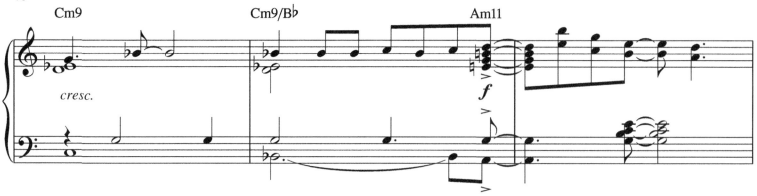

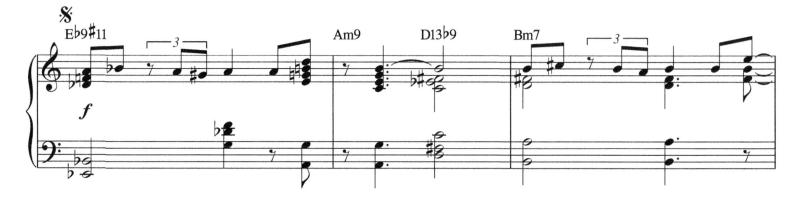

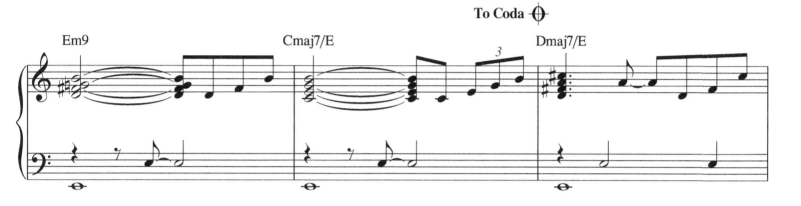

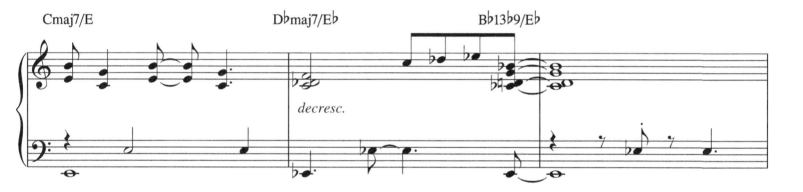

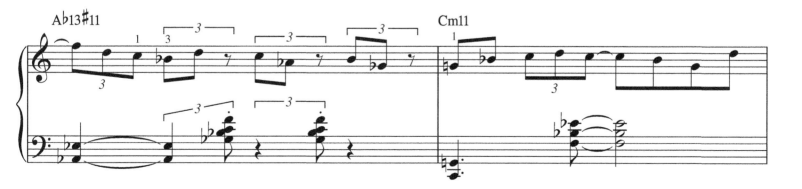

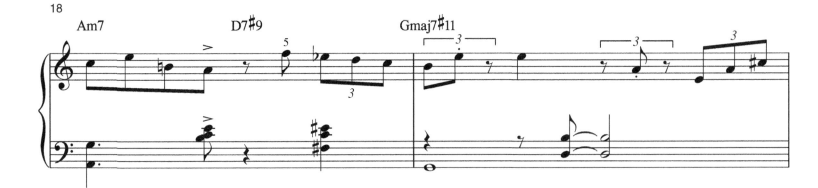

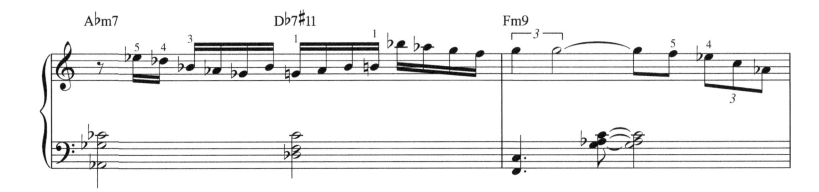

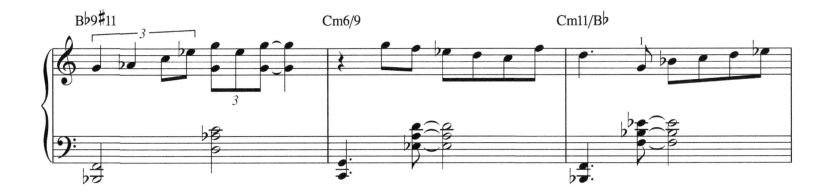

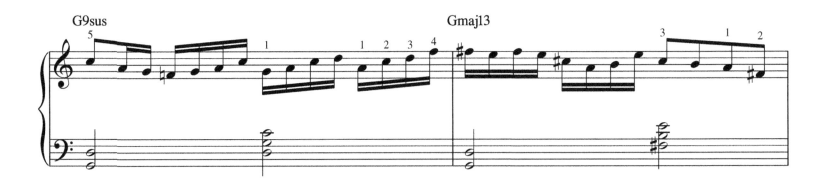

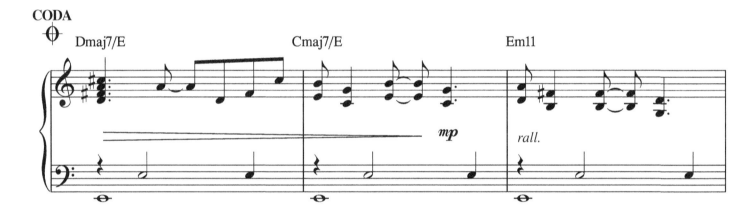

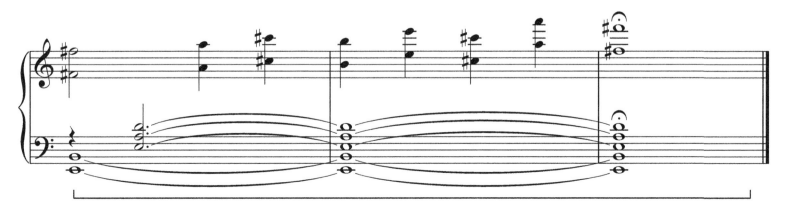

DUKE'S PLACE

Words and Music by DUKE ELLINGTON,
WILLIAM KATZ, ROBERT THIELE
and RUTH ROBERTS

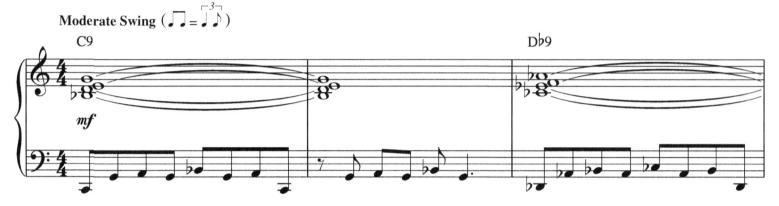

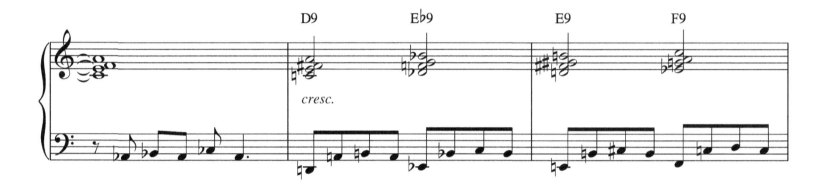

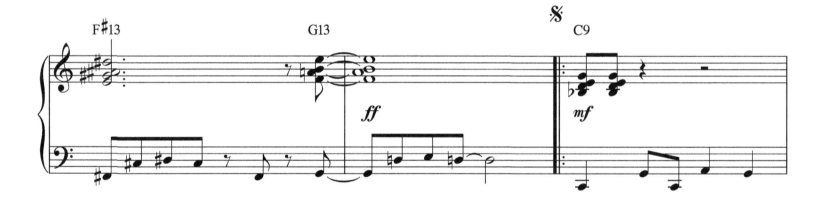

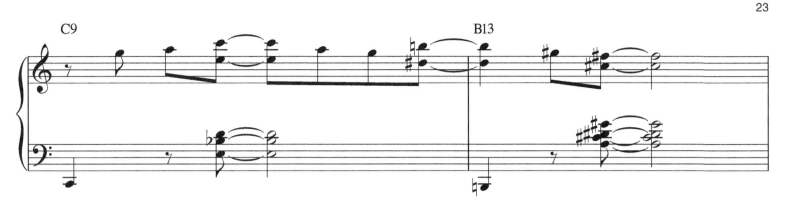

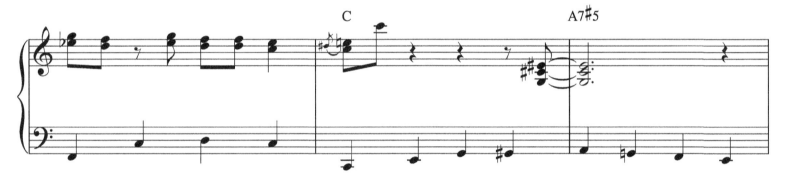

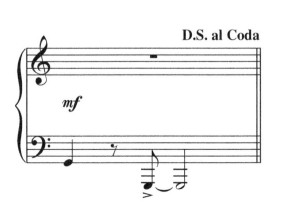

FILTHY McNASTY

Words and Music by
HORACE SILVER

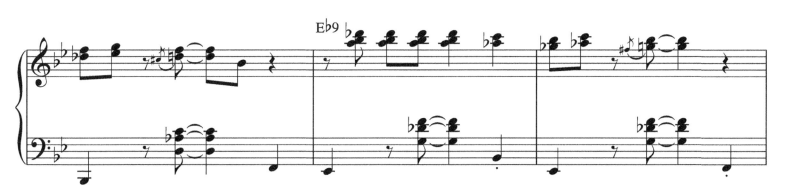

GINGER BREAD BOY

By JIMMY HEATH

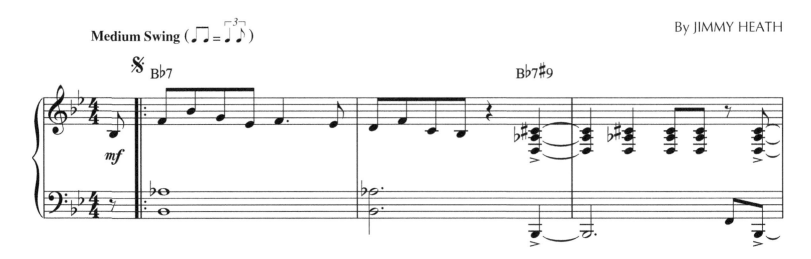

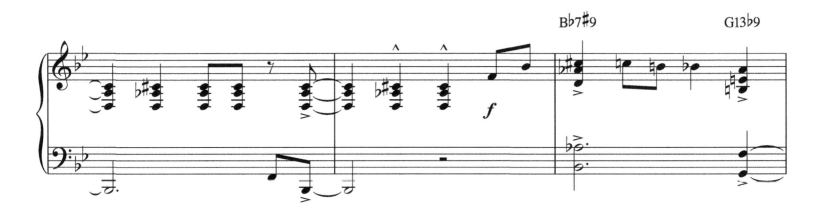

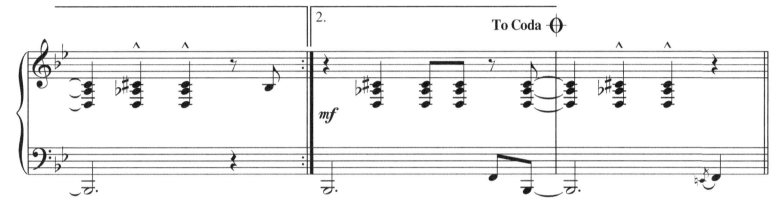

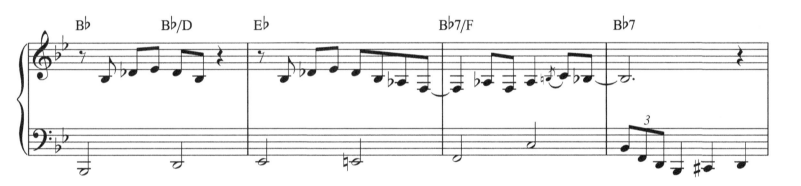

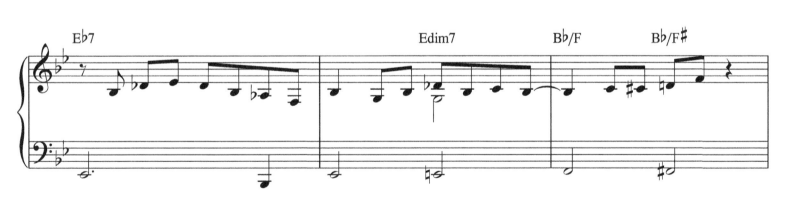

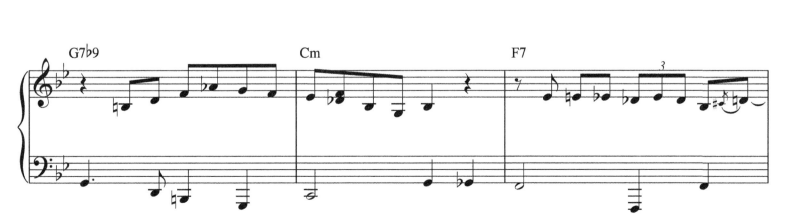

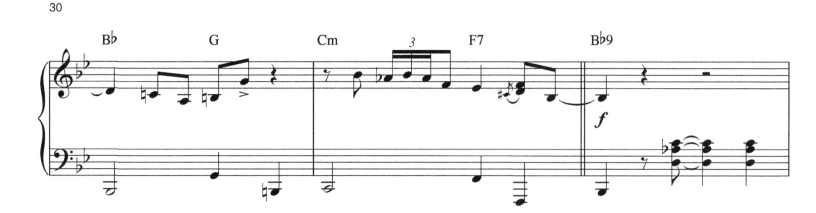

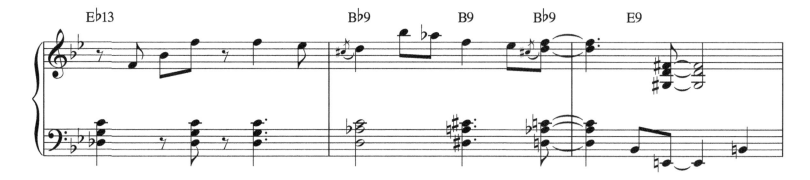

D.S. al Coda

CODA

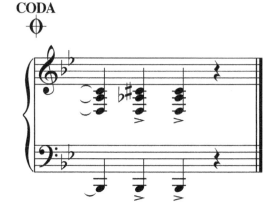

GOOD BAIT

By TADD DAMERON
and COUNT BASIE

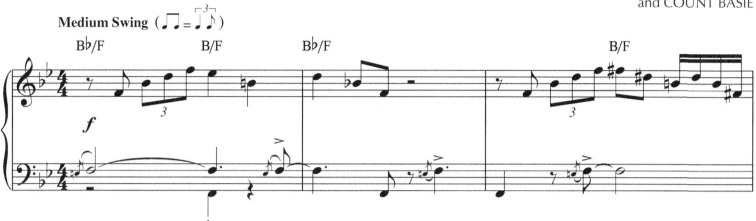

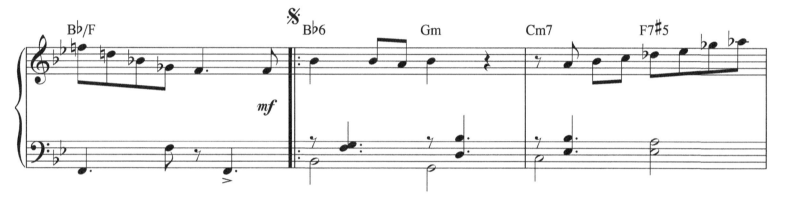

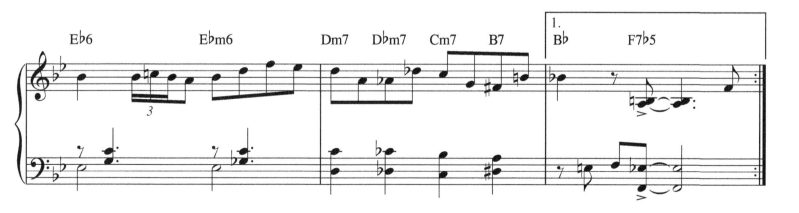

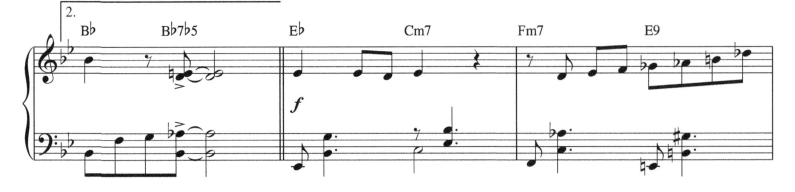

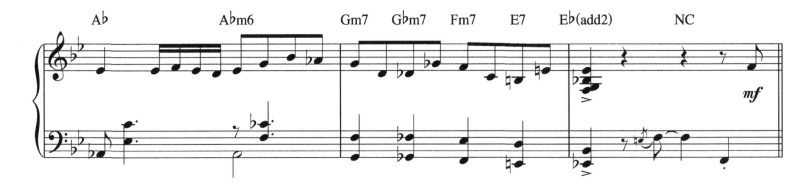

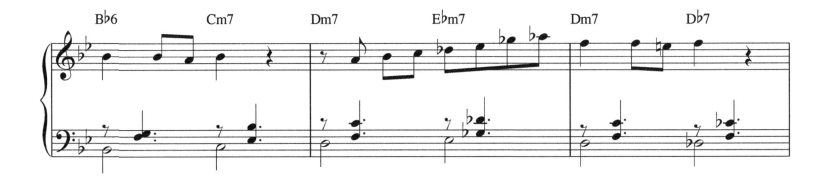

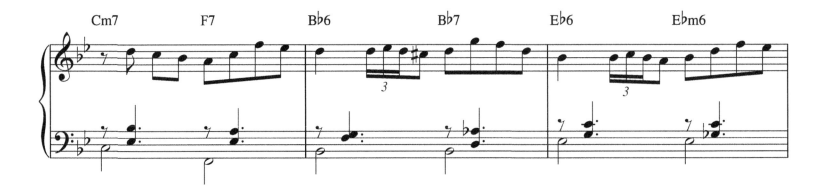

To Coda ⊕

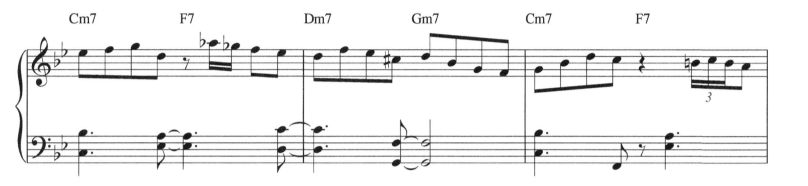

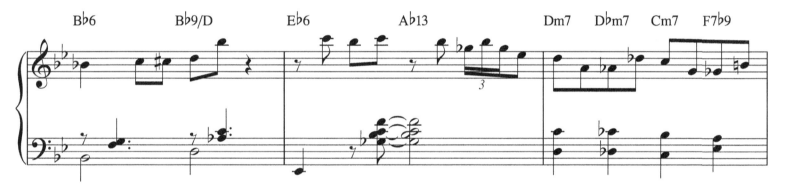

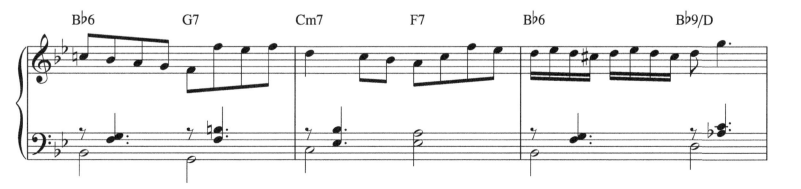

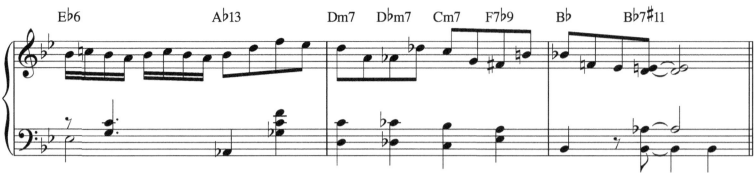

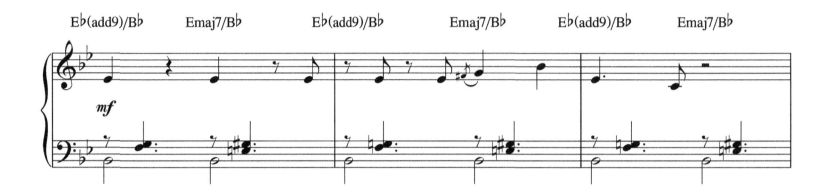

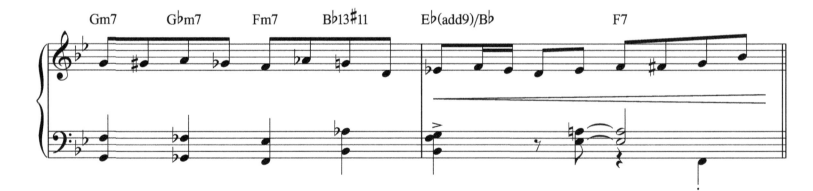

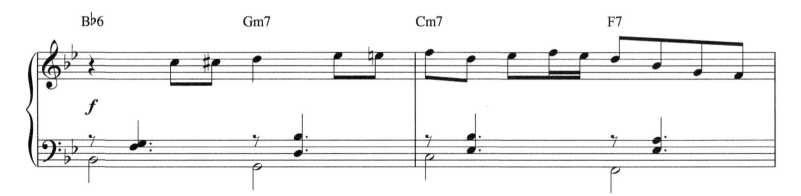

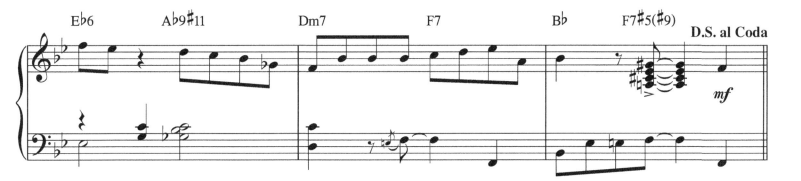

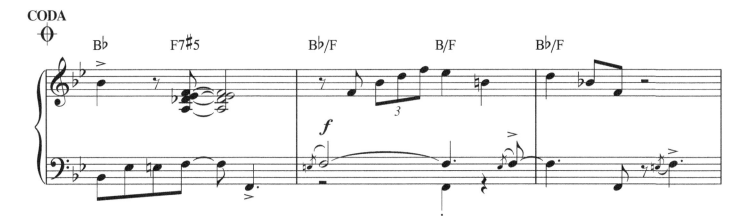

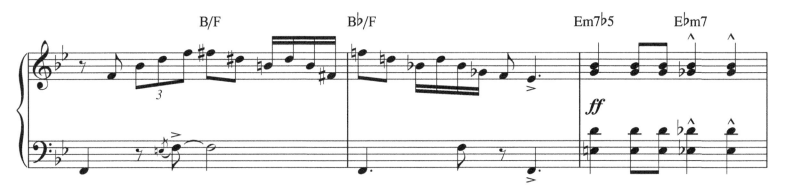

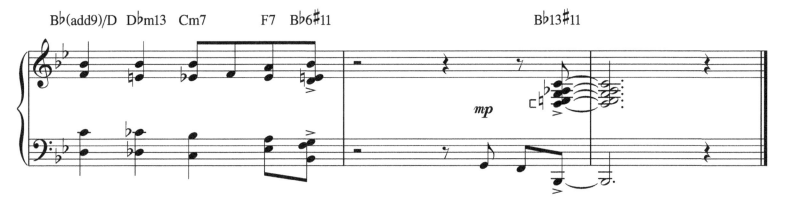

HOT HOUSE

By TADD DAMERON

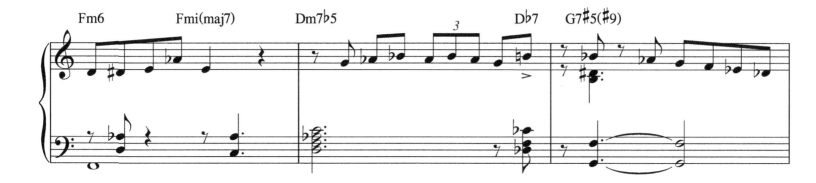

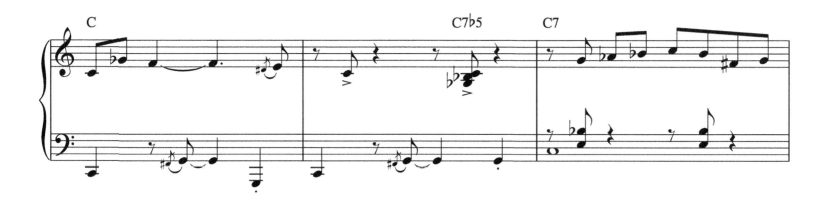

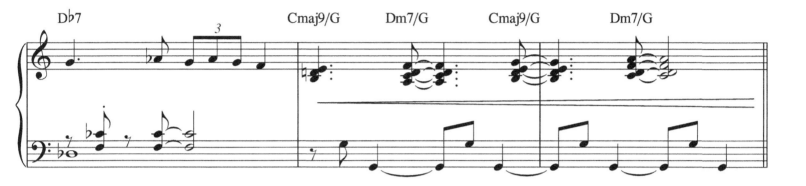

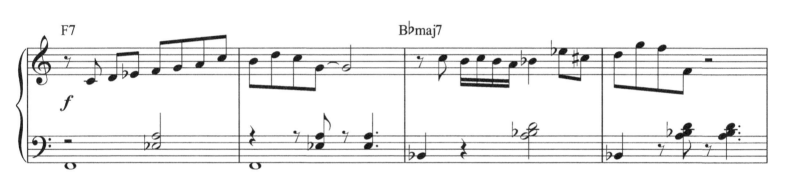

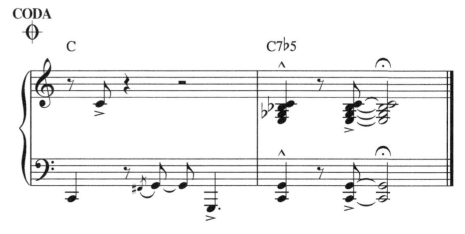

IN YOUR OWN SWEET WAY

By DAVE BRUBECK

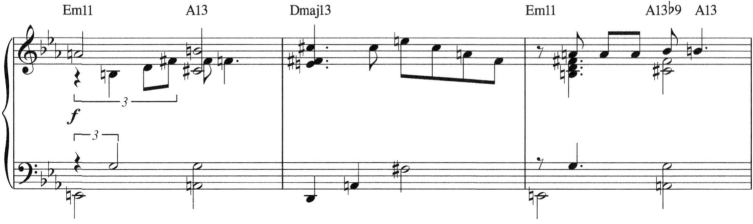

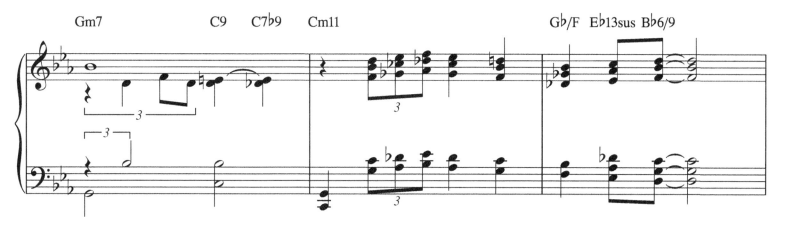

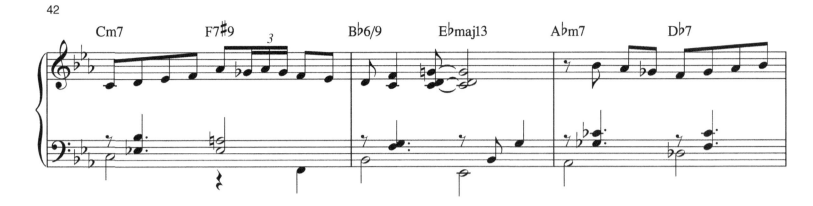

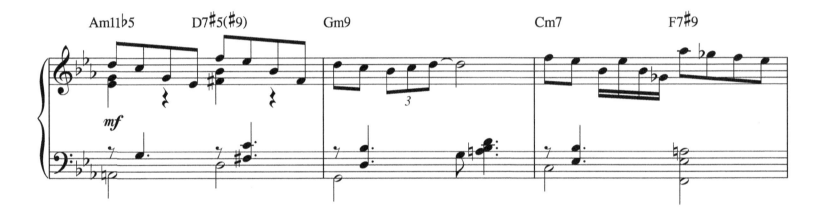

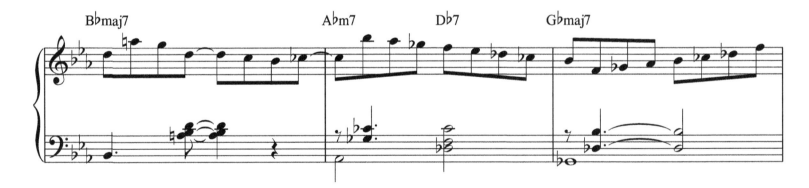

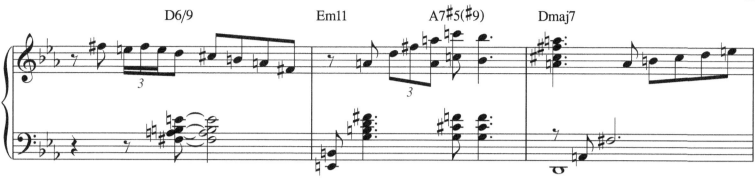

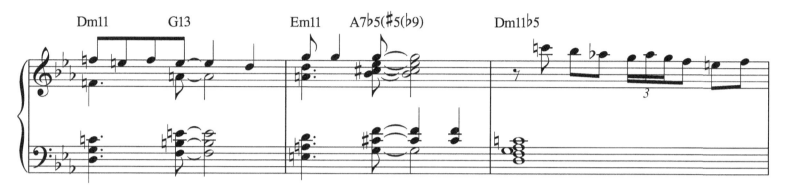

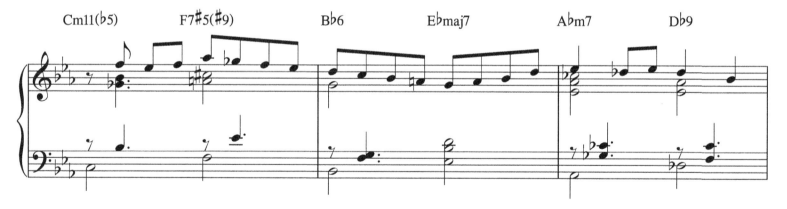

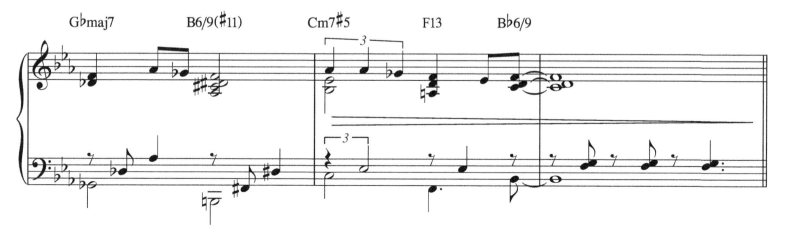

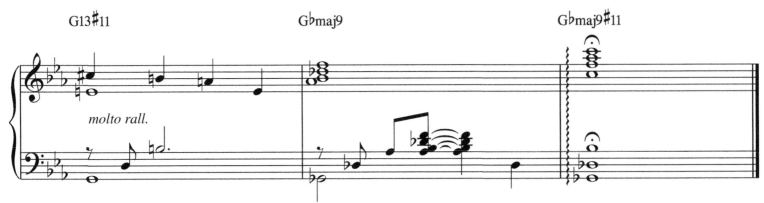

LADY DAY

By WAYNE SHORTER

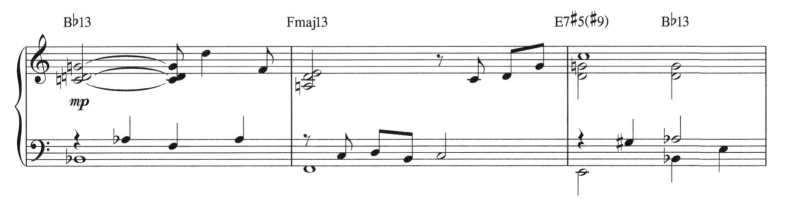

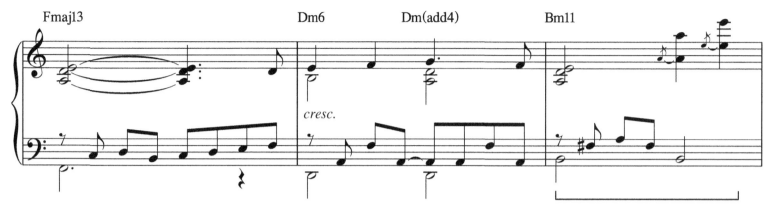

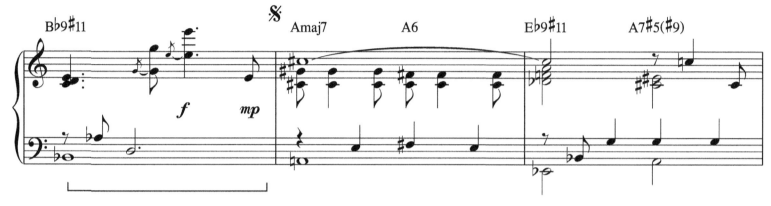

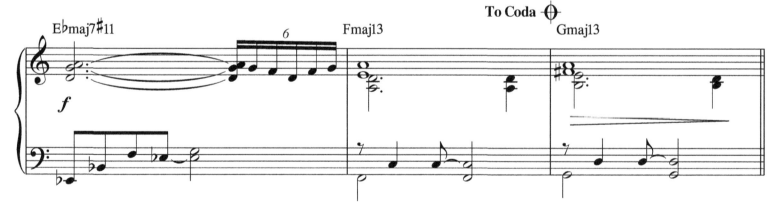

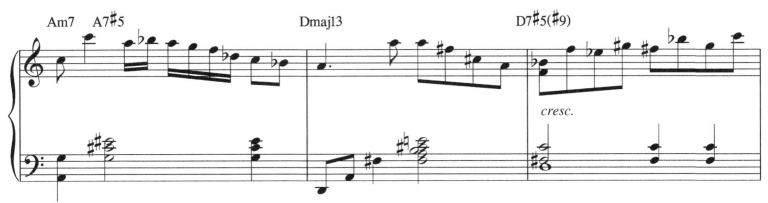

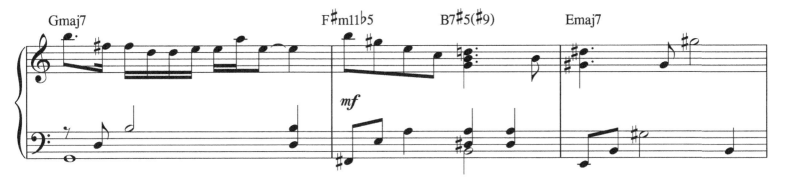

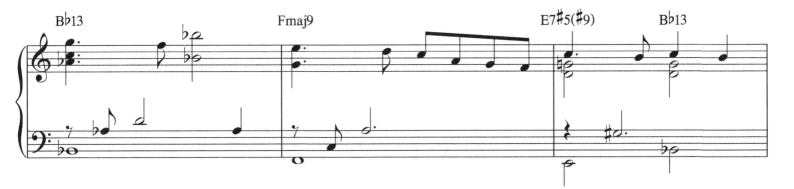

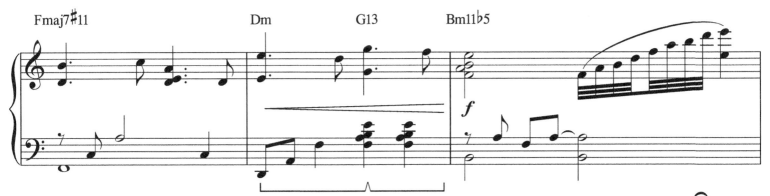

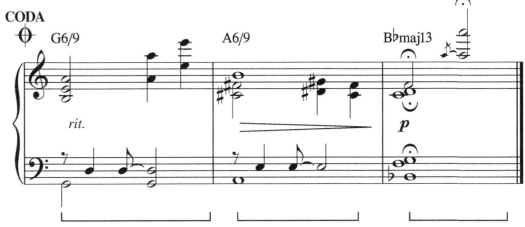

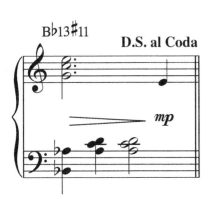

ISFAHAN
from FAR EAST SUITE

By DUKE ELLINGTON
and BILLY STRAYHORN

Ballad

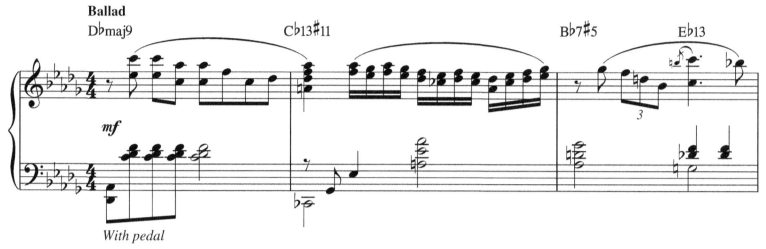

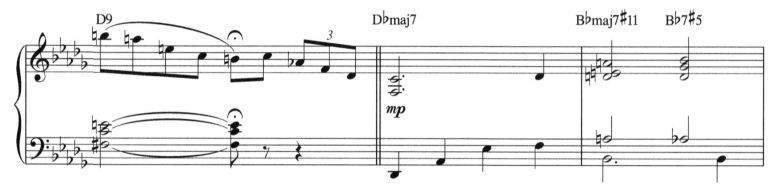

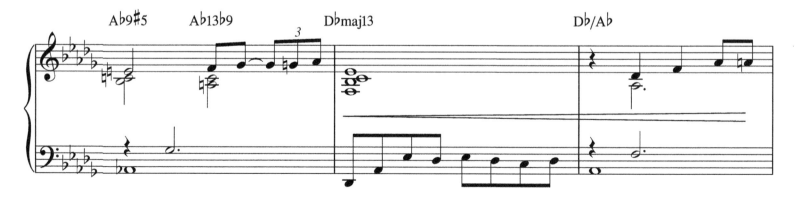

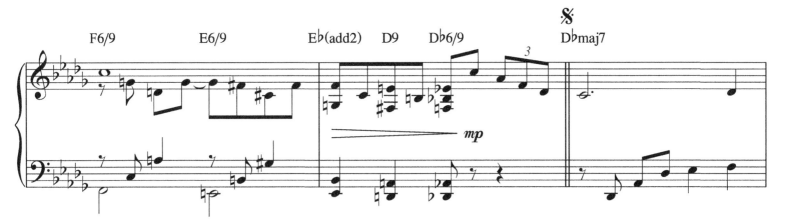

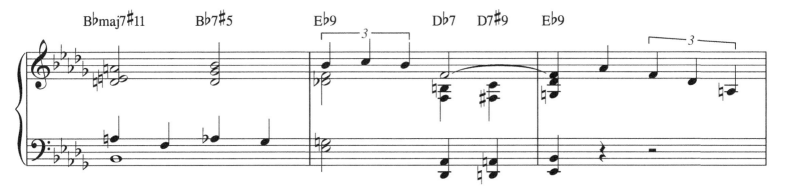

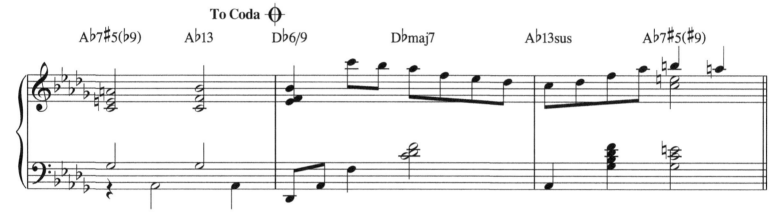

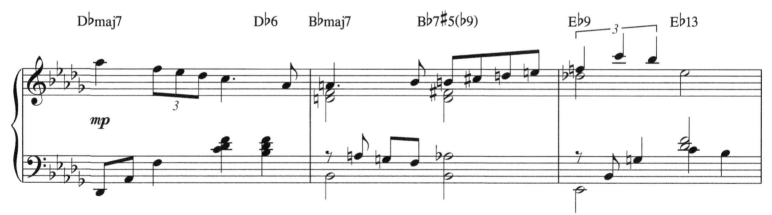

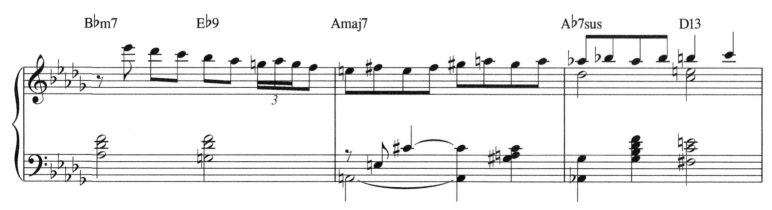

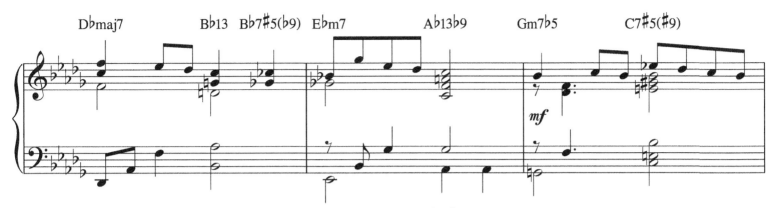

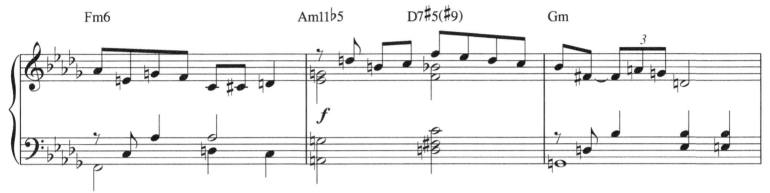

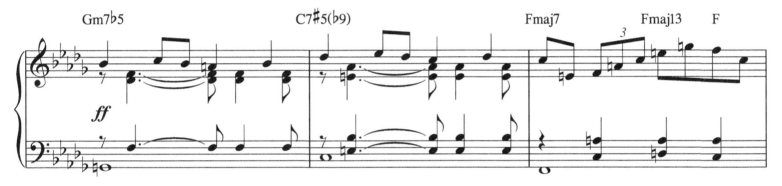

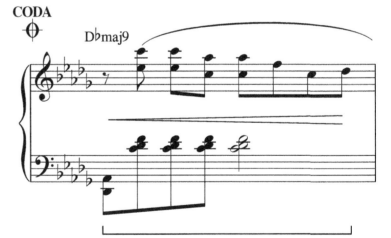

MINOR MOOD

By BARNEY KESSEL

Medium Swing

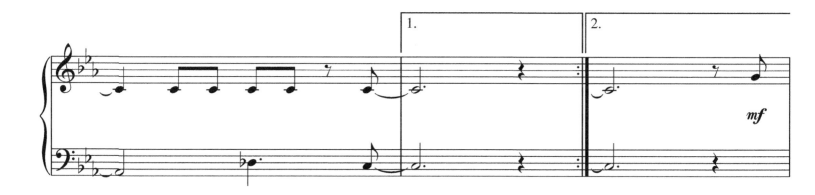

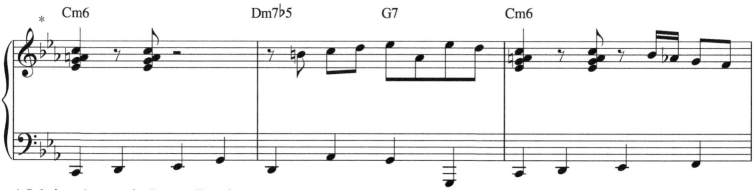

Solo based on one by Barney Kessel.

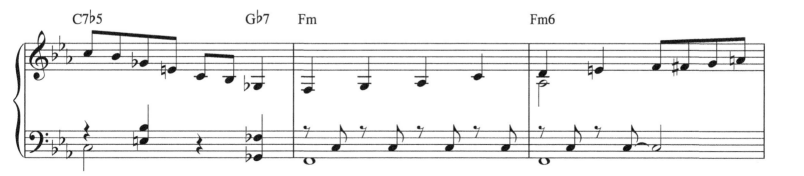

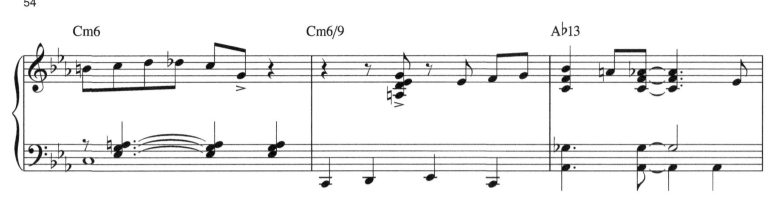

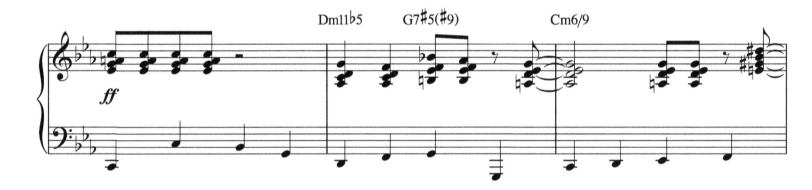

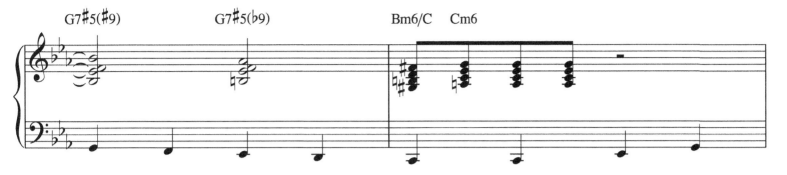

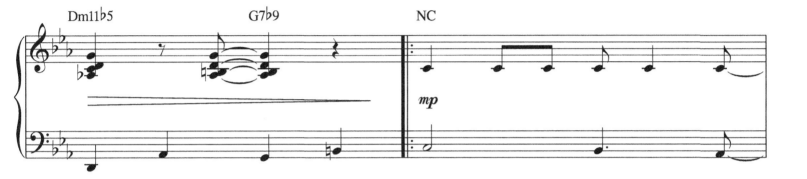

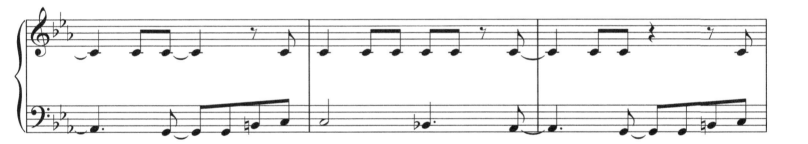

MINOR SWING

By DJANGO REINHARDT
and STEPHANE GRAPPELLI

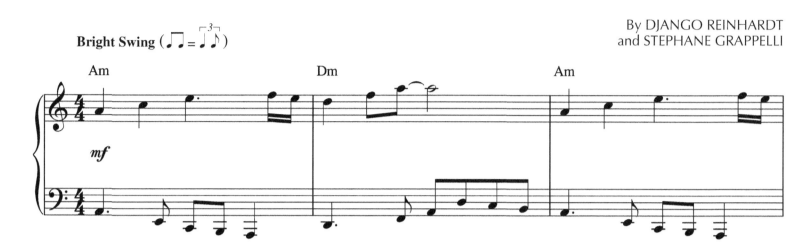

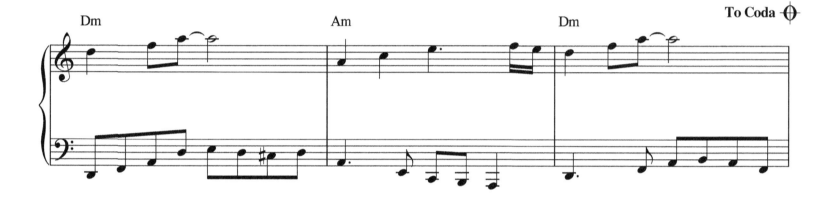

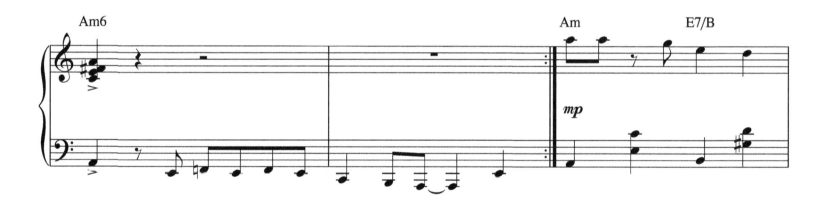

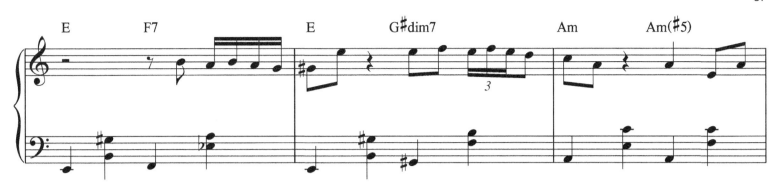

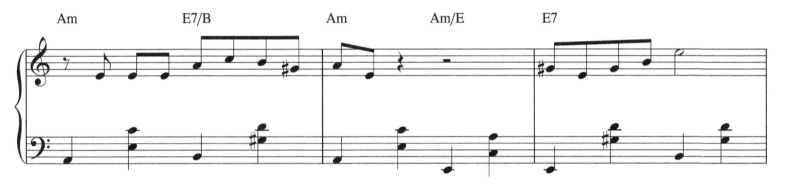

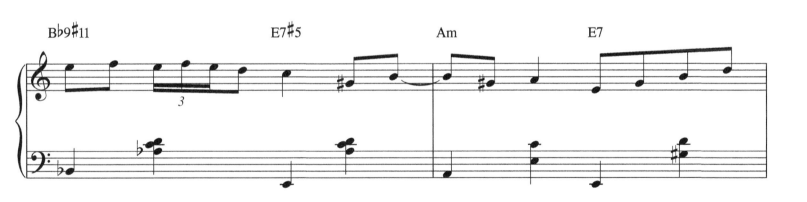

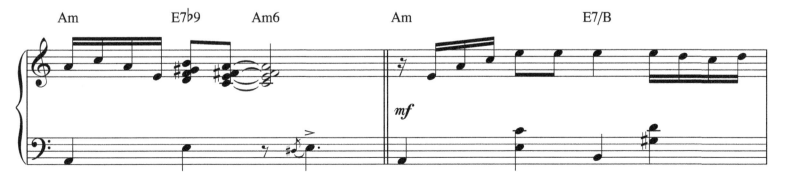

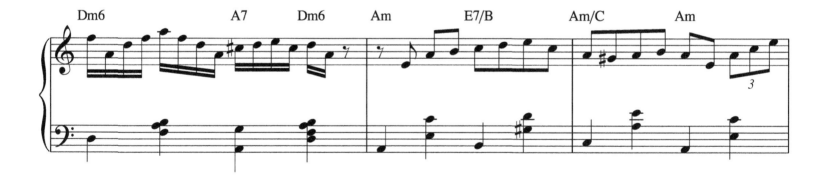

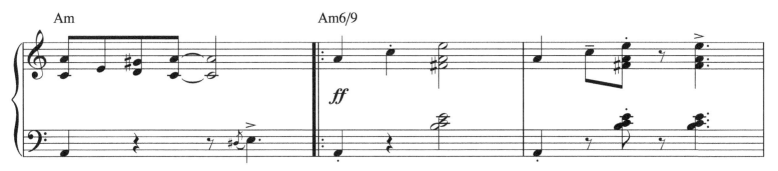

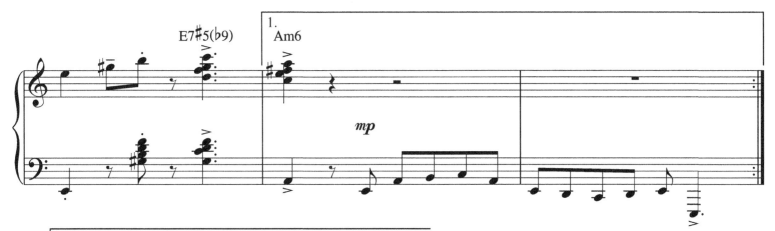

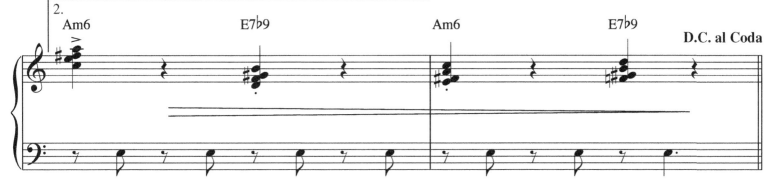

OUR DELIGHT

By TADD DAMERON

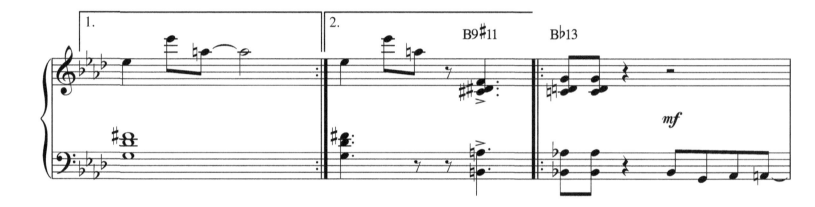

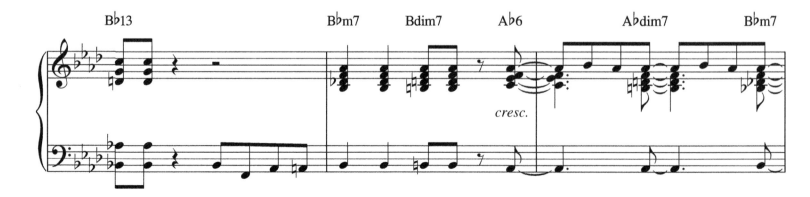

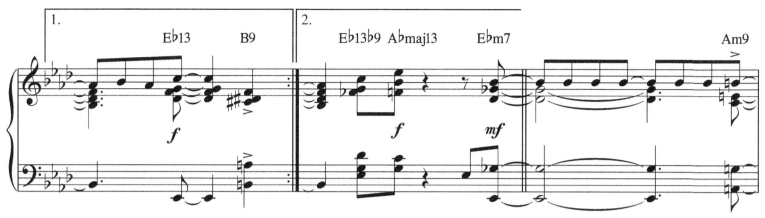

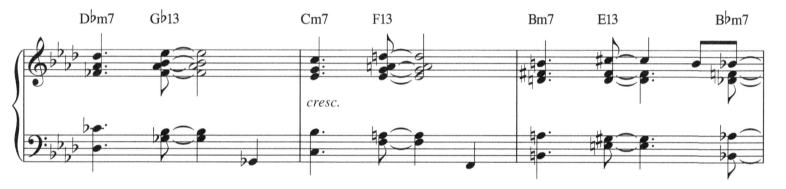

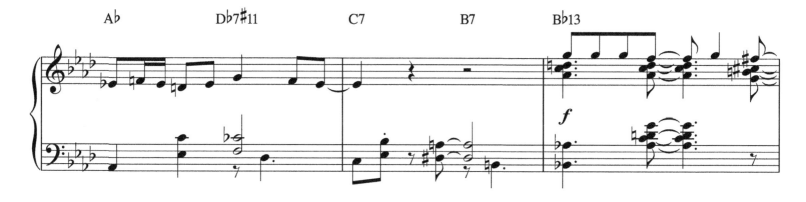

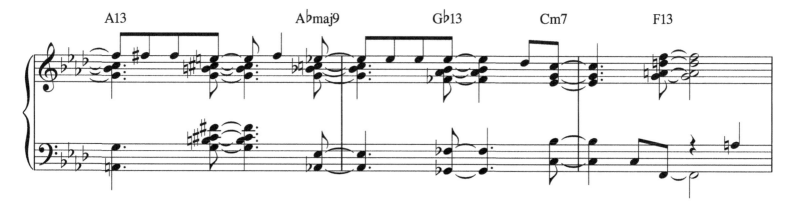

PENT UP HOUSE

By SONNY ROLLINS

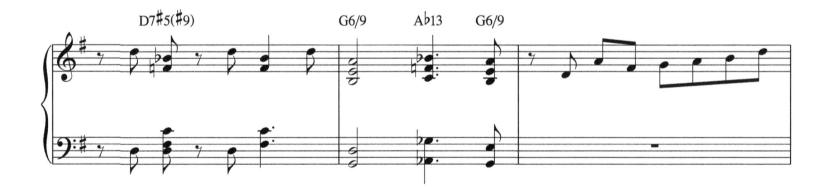

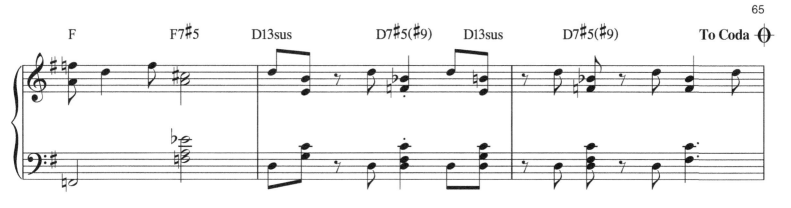

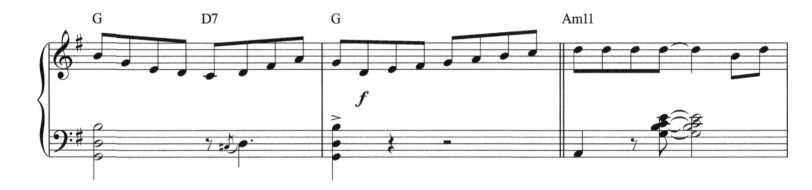

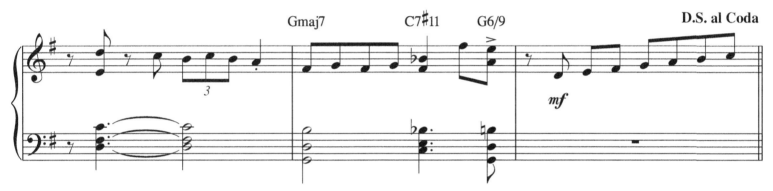

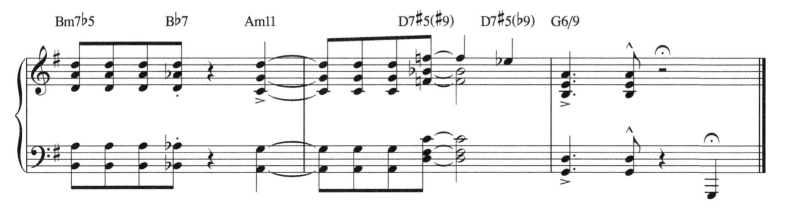

RIFFTIDE

By COLEMAN HAWKINS

Medium Swing

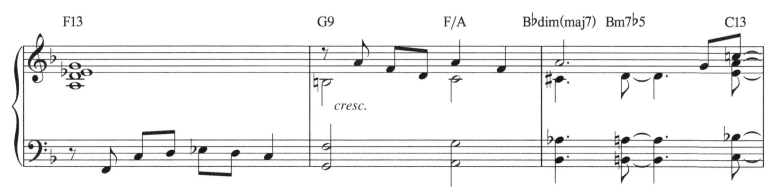

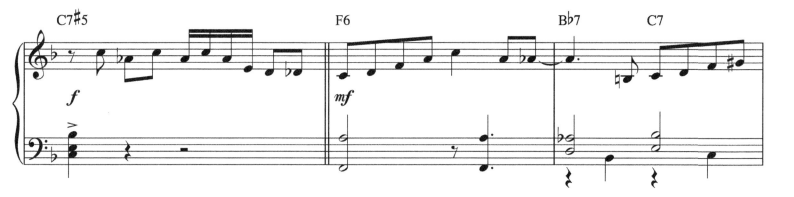

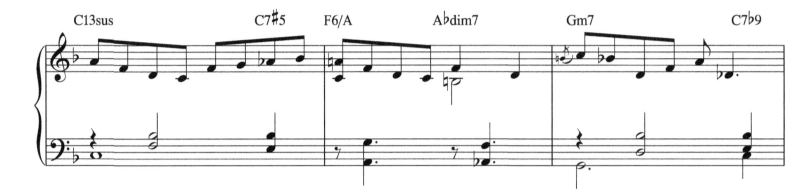

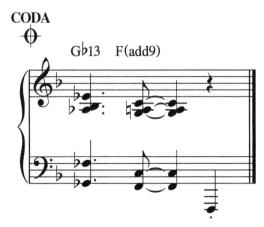

ROAD SONG

By JOHN L. (WES) MONTGOMERY

Moderate Rock

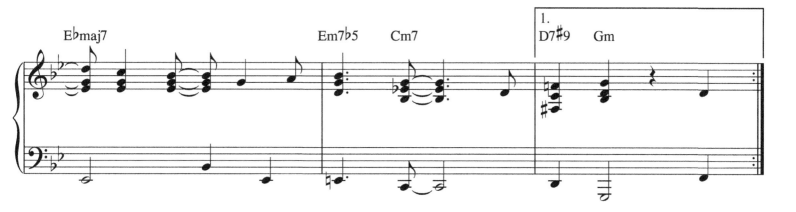

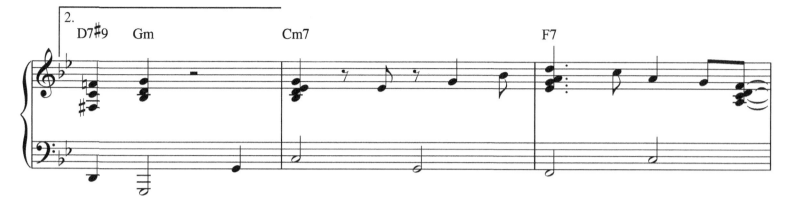

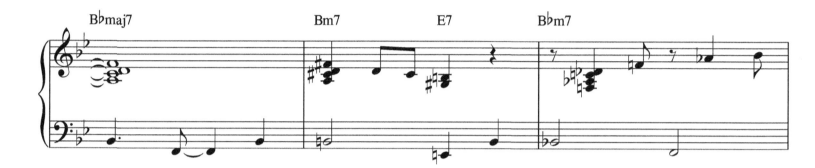

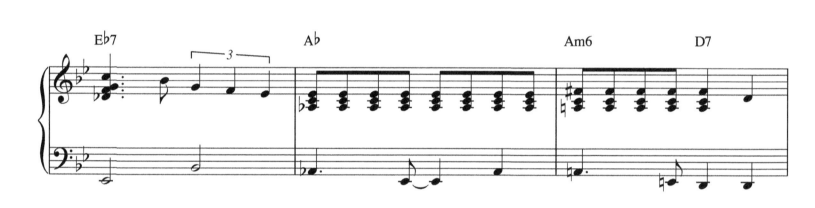

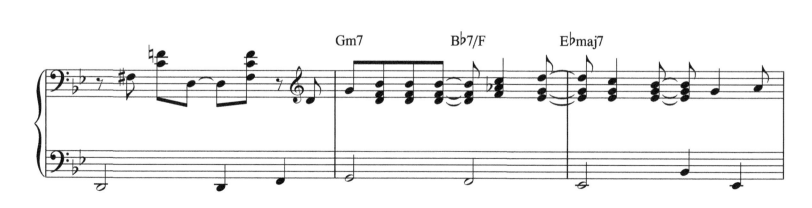

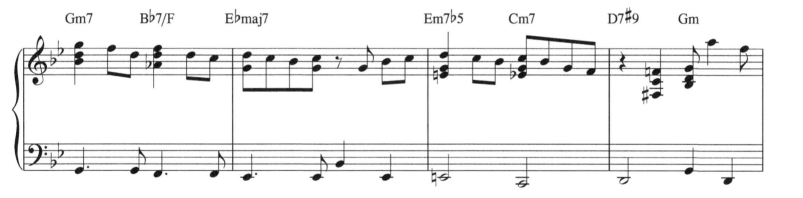

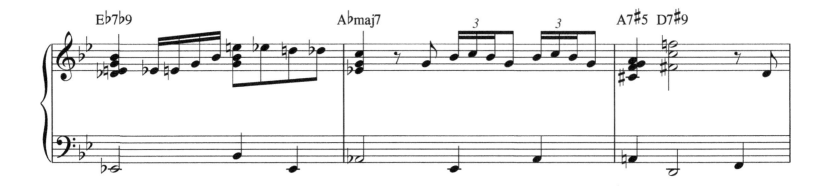

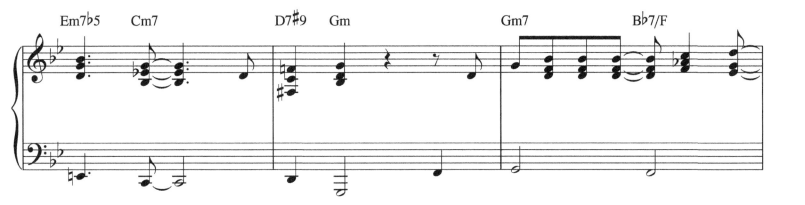

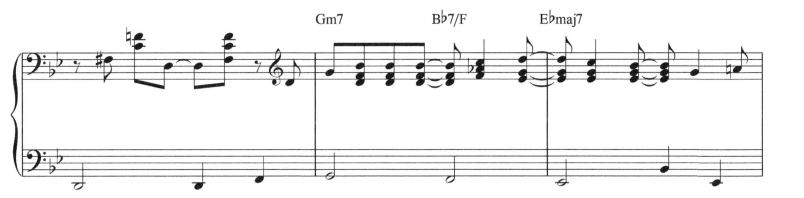

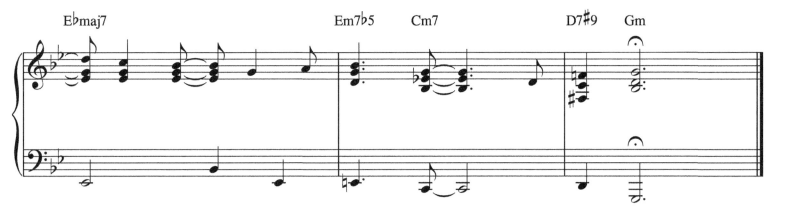

STAR EYES

Words by DON RAYE
Music by GENE DePAUL

Bossa Nova

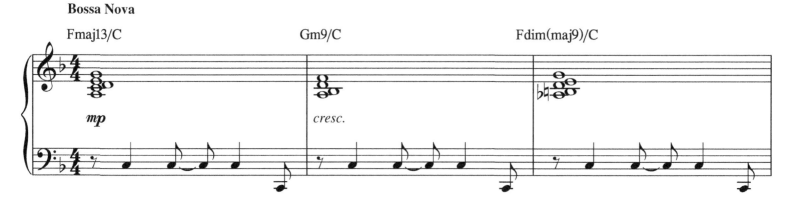

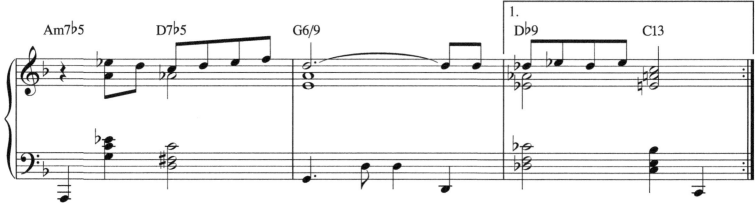

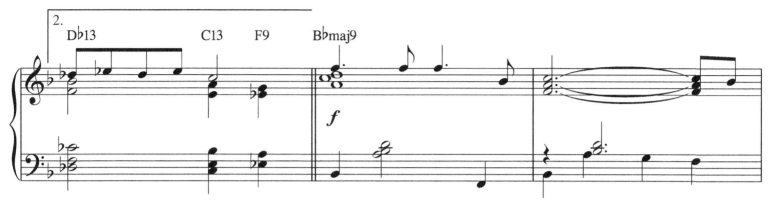

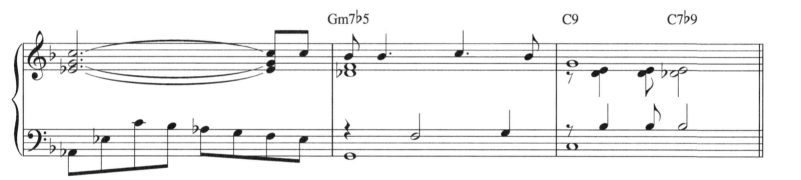

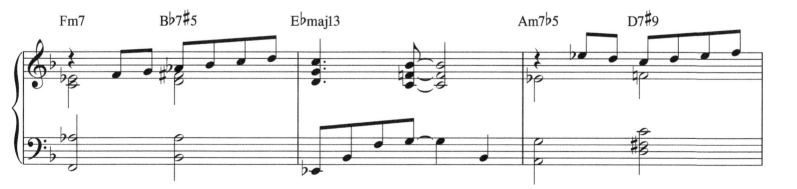

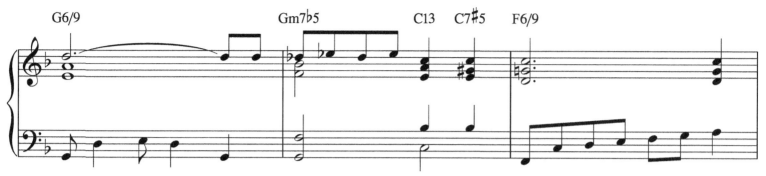

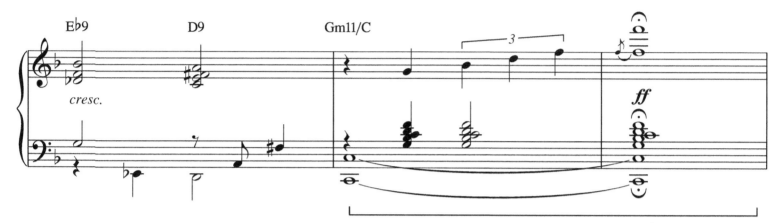

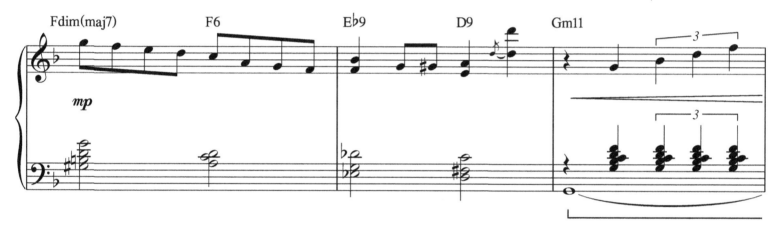

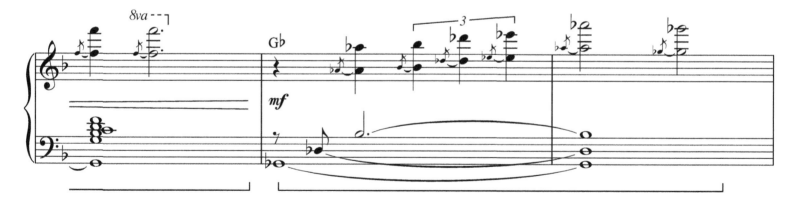

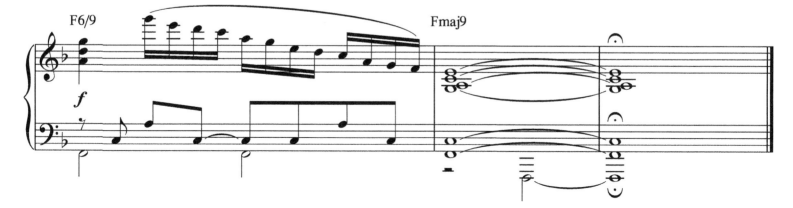

UN POCO LOCO

By EARL "BUD" POWELL

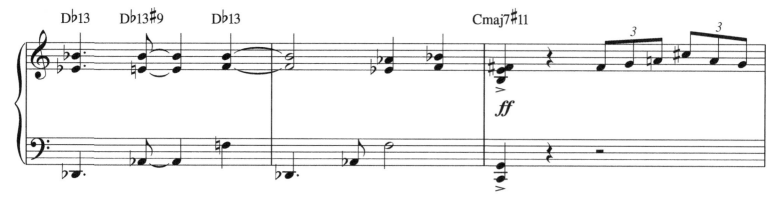

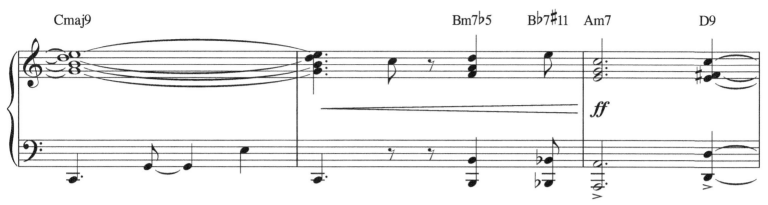

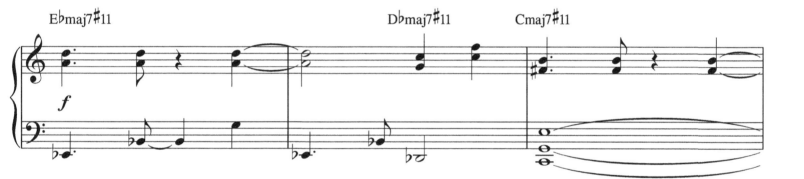

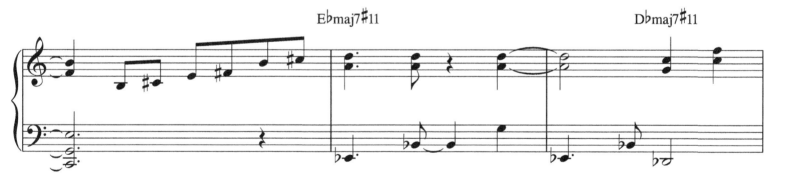

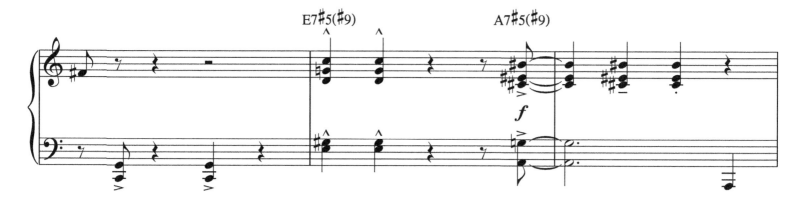

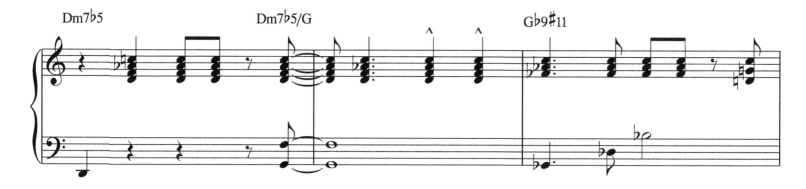

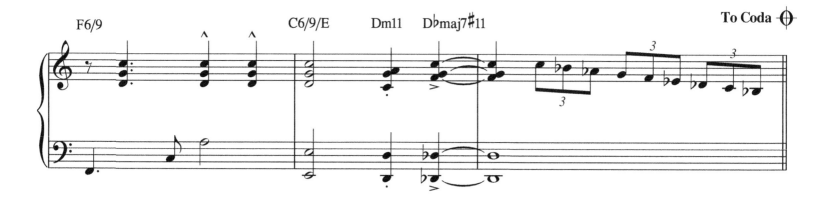

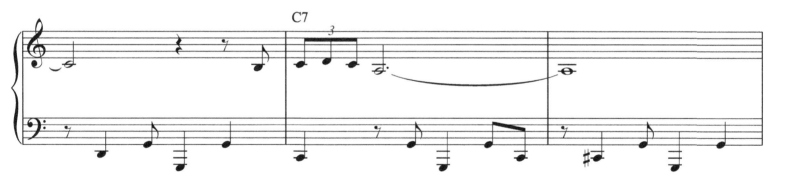

D.S. al Coda
(repeat only for improvisation)

CODA

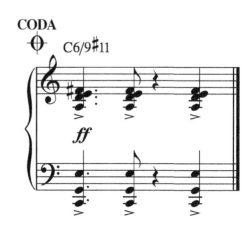

VALSE HOT

By SONNY ROLLINS

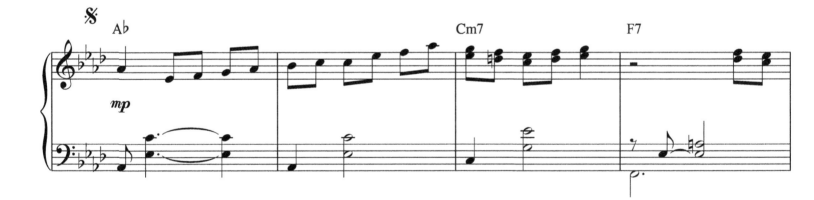

To Coda ⊕

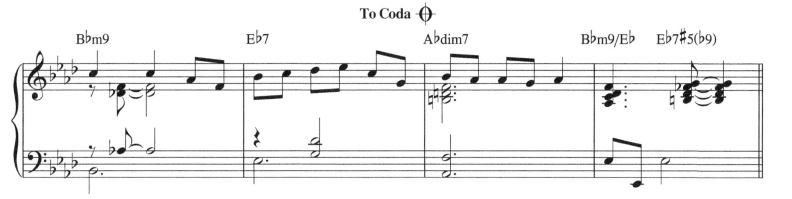

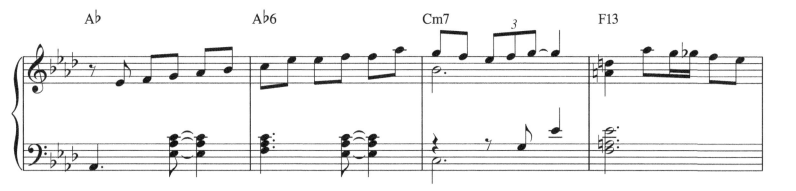

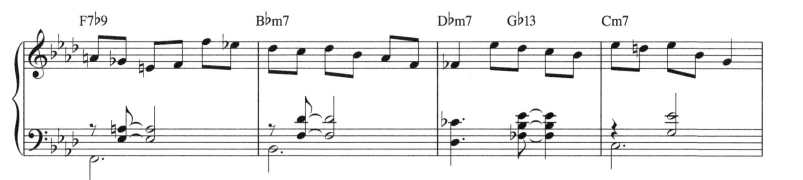

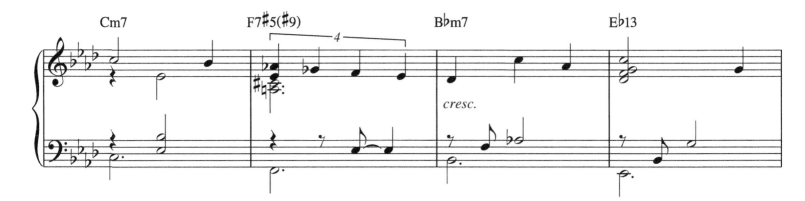

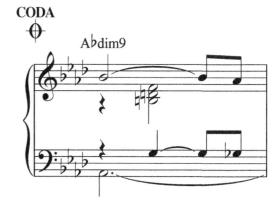

WATERMELON MAN

By HERBIE HANCOCK

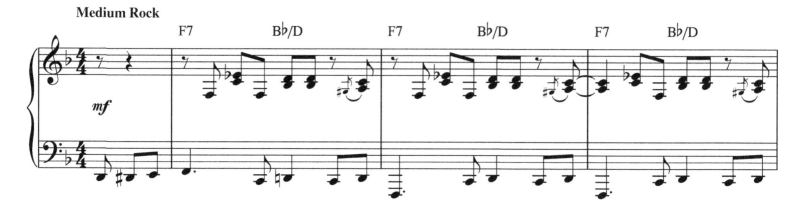

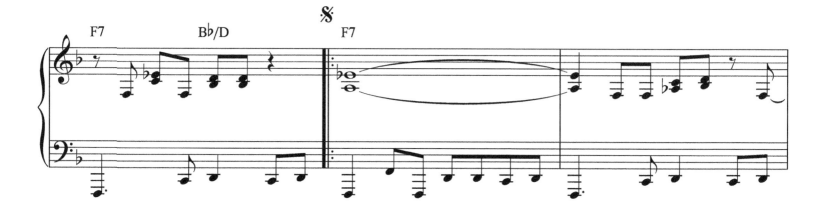

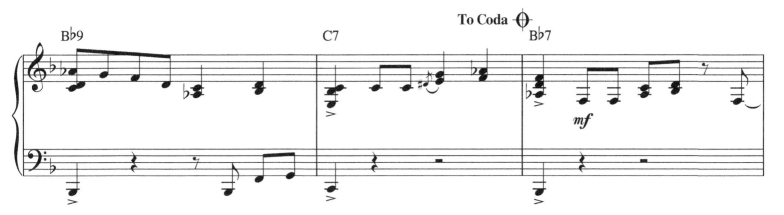

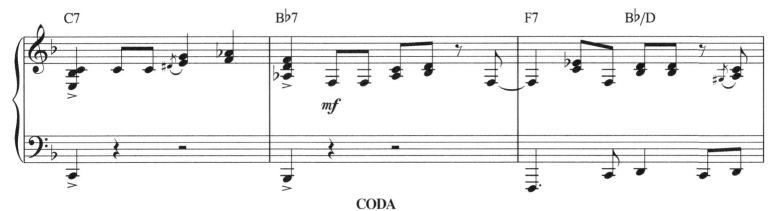

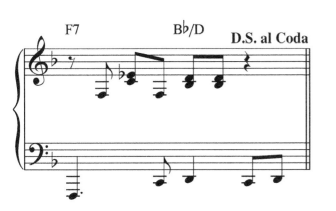

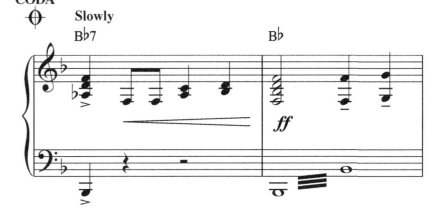

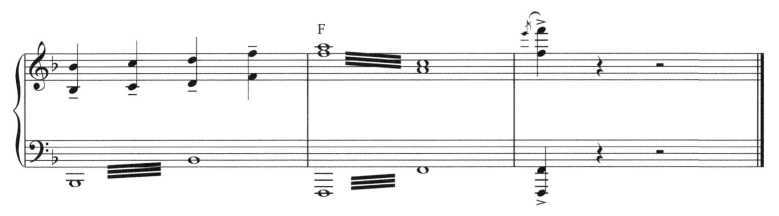

UP JUMPED SPRING

By FREDDIE HUBBARD

Medium Jazz Waltz

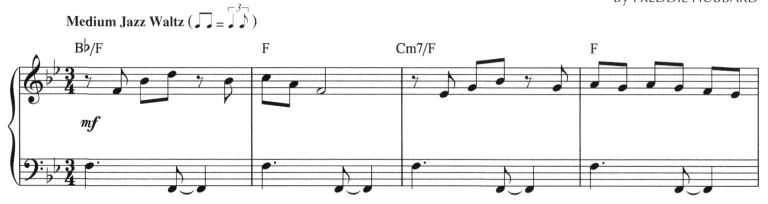

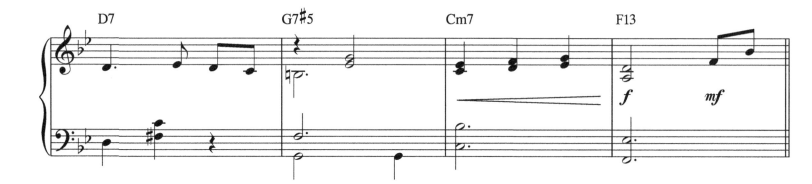

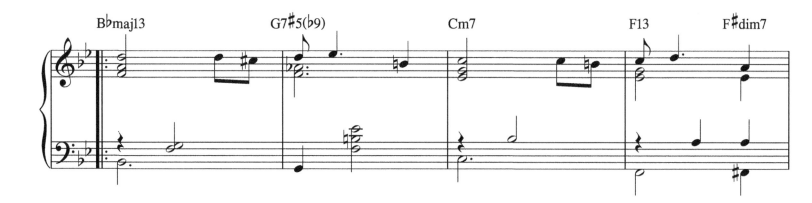

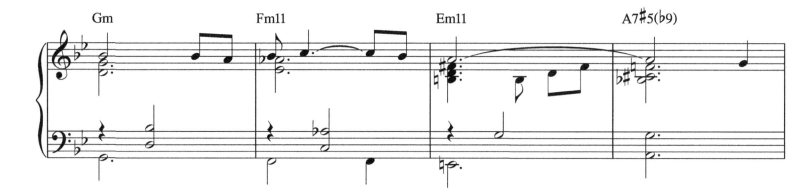

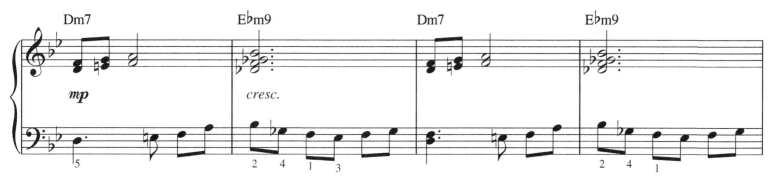

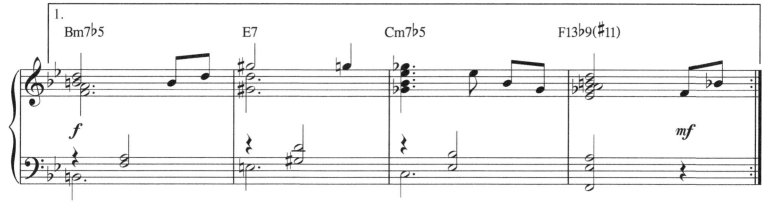

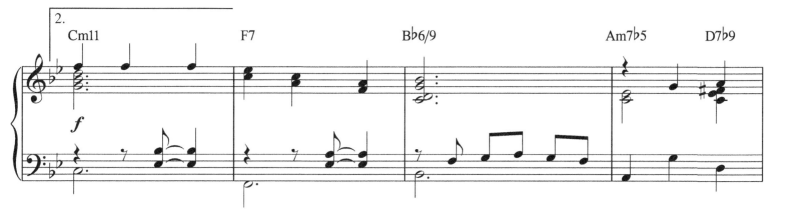

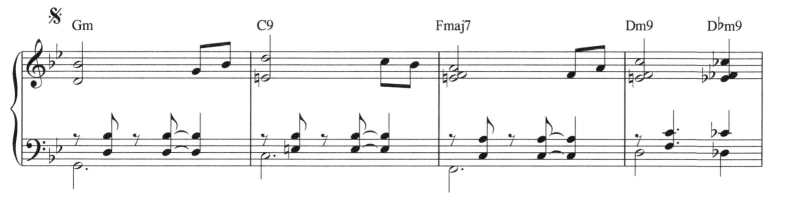

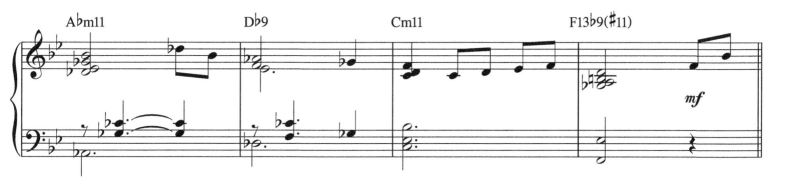

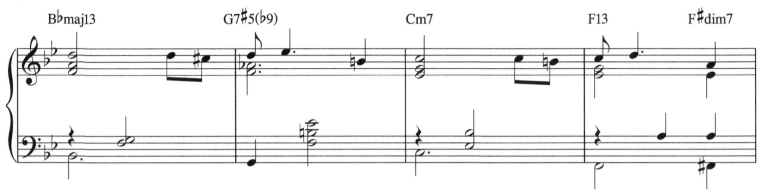

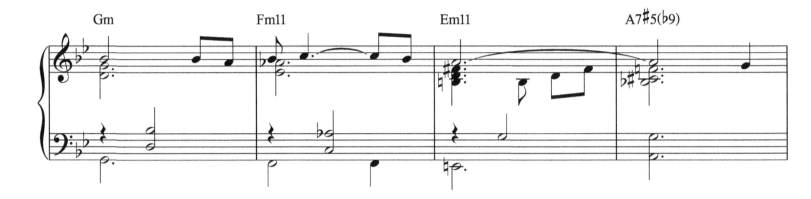

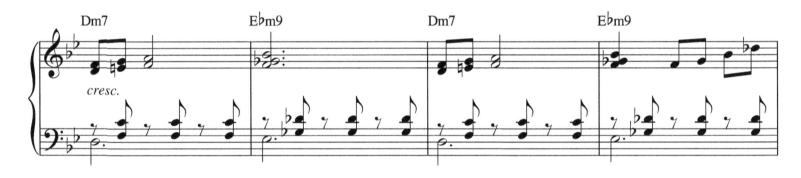

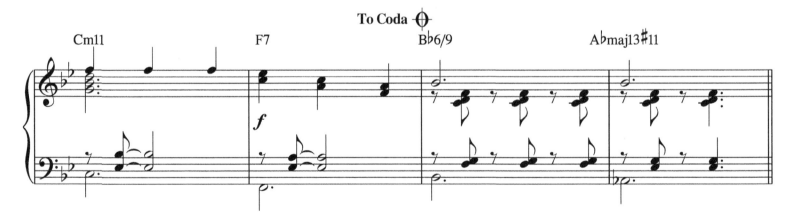

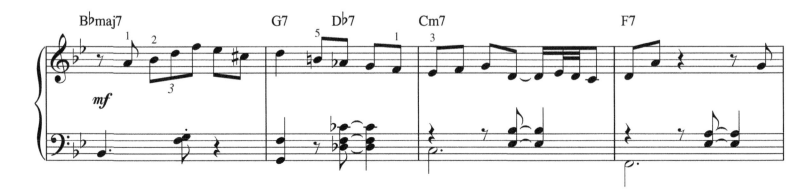

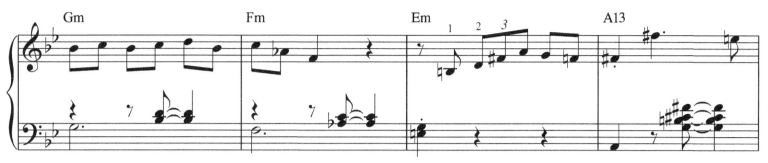

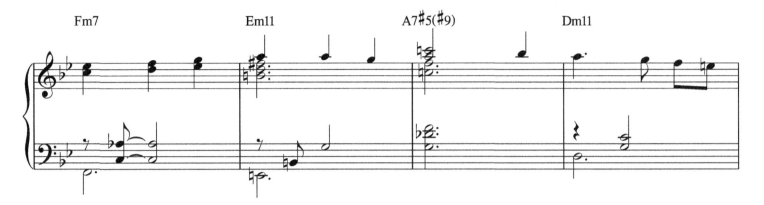

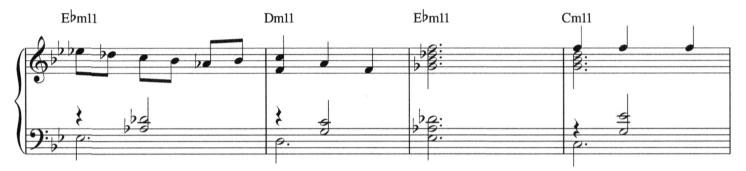

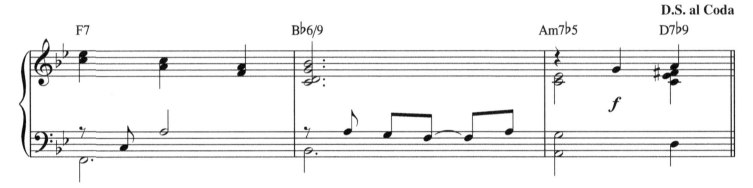

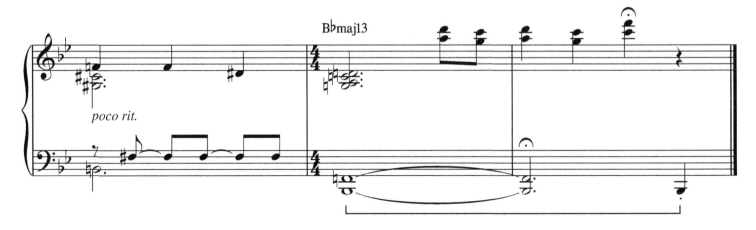